D0119648

YOUR COUNTRY NEEDS YOU

This book is dedicated to the memory of the men of The Lincolnshire Regiment who died in the First World War and, in particular, to my uncle, Sergeant Andrew Crick, C Company, 1st/4th Battalion, wounded by a 'whizz-bang' at Sanctuary Wood, died on 5 October 1915 at No.10 Casualty Clearing Station at Remi Farm near Poperinghe and buried, according to the Belgian priest who officiated, 'in the little cemetery which is near our hospital'. His grave is now in Plot 1, Row B, of what was once known as Remi Siding Cemetery, now called Lijssenthoek Miliary Cemetery with 9,882 graves of British and Empire servicemen and women.

YOUR COUNTRY
NEEDS YOU

From Six to Sixty-Five Divisions

MARTIN
MIDDLEBROOK

Pen & Sword Books Limited, Barnsley
LEO COOPER

Other books by Martin Middlebrook

The First Day on the Somme
The Nuremberg Raid
Convoy
Battleship (*with Patrick Mahoney*)
The Kaiser's Battle
The Battle Hamburg
The Peenemünde Raid
The Schweinfurt-Regensburg Mission
The Bomber Command War Diaries (*with Chris Everitt*)
Operation Corporate (*in paperback as* Task Force)
The Berlin Raids
The Fight for the 'Malvinas'
The Somme Battlefields (*with Mary Middlebrook*)
Arnhem 1944

Photographs by kind permission of the Taylor Library
Picture research by Roni Wilkinson

First published in Great Britain in 2000 by Leo Cooper
an imprint of Pen & Sword Books Limited
47 Church Street, Barnsley, South Yorkshire S70 2AS

Copyright © Martin Middlebrook, 2000

For up-to date information on other titles produced under the Pen & Sword imprint,
please telephone or write to:
Pen & Sword Books Limited
FREEPOST
47 Church Street
Barnsley
South Yorkshire
S70 2BR

Telephone (24 hours): 01226 734555

ISBN 0-85052-711-2 – cased edition
    0-85052-709-0 – paperback edition

All rights reserved. No part of this publication may be reproduced, stored in a retrieval system, or transmitted,
in any form or by any means, electronic, mechanical, photocopying, recording or otherwise, without prior
permission from the publishers. This book is sold subject to the condition that it shall not, by way of trade or
otherwise, be lent, resold, hired out, or otherwise circulated without the publisher's prior consent in any form of
binding or cover other than that in which it is published and without a similiar condition, including this
condition, being imposed on the subsequent purchaser.

British Library Cataloguing in Publication Data

Printed by Redwood Books Ltd
Trowbridge, Wiltshire

Contents

The last few weeks of peace – George V inspecting a guard of honour drawn up to receive him at Perth, July 1914. The spark for world conflict had already flashed up the previous month.

Introduction

At 11.00 pm on 4 August 1914, Great Britain declared herself to be at war with Germany because of that country's refusal to respect Belgian neutrality, a neutrality which Britain was pledged by an old treaty to guarantee. Britain thus found herself among the great powers of Europe in her first experience of continental warfare since Wellington defeated Napoleon on a Belgian battlefield almost a century earlier. Britain was certainly one of those great powers in 1914 but, whereas the status of other major combatant countries was backed by armies based on universal male conscription, Britain's world position was based on the Royal Navy and her worldwide Empire. The small British Army was made up of volunteer soldiers and was little more than an imperial police force when compared to the conscription armies.

From Six to Sixty-Five is the title of a talk I regularly give to military-minded groups. I thought that my writing career was over with the completion of fourteen full-length books and set out to do no more with this subject than fill some empty winter days by turning into written form my description of how Britain expanded that small 1914 army so

Archduke Franz Ferdinand and his wife on their final journey through the streets of Sarajevo, 28 June 1914. Following their assassination, Austria blamed Serbia for the murder of their heir to the throne. Russia backed Serbia, Germany backed Austria, France supported Russia.

dramatically in the hope that a small, privately published book might ensue. But the work came out at greater length than expected and I am grateful to Pen and Sword Books Limited for offering to publish it in commercial form. That expansion of the British Army during the First World War was, I believe, one of the unsung achievements of our country in that war. I start my talks by stating that army divisions are the 'units of currency' of nations at war. A country's influence on the battlefield and in any post-war settlement, providing it finishes on the winning side, is in direct proportion to the number of divisions it can put into the field.

Britain started that new war with just six infantry divisions and the equivalent of one cavalry division available at home for immediate action; the remainder of the Army was stationed at overseas garrisons. If Britain wanted to be a major combatant in the coming war, that small force at

Germany's strategic plan for war with France required the violation of Belgian neutrality. The assassins had unwittingly started a disastrous chain of events. Arrest of Cabrinovitz one of the assassins.

In 1839 the then British Prime Minister, Lord Palmerston, signed a treaty guaranteeing Belgium's independence. His signature on that paper, alongside the seal of Great Britain, was published as encouragement to the British people to view the declaration of war against Germany as a just and righteous act.

home would have to be expanded several times. There was, in theory, an alternative. Britain was not directly threatened in 1914. In order to fulfil her treaty obligation to Belgium and the military understanding she had with France, Britain might have contributed those immediately available six divisions and then sent no more. Portugal, later in the war, satisfied her honour by sending just two divisions.

But that was not the British way. Britain had been the main means of defeating Napoleon in 1815. In my lifetime she would later join wholeheartedly in the Second World War, in the Korean War and in the Gulf War. She would mobilize a task force to turn Argentine invaders out of a remote British possession deep in the South Atlantic in 1982. In 1914 Britain could think of doing nothing other than partaking with her utmost effort in defeating the Kaiser and Germany's ambition to dominate Europe. It is a sad thought that these honourable sentiments have filled military cemeteries around the world with the graves of young British servicemen. (I am writing this paragraph in June 1999 when British troops are providing a large part of the ground forces entering Kosovo following the eleven-week NATO bombing of Serbia, the entire operation undertaken largely on a British initiative.)

So I will try to put on paper the story of how Britain raised a continental-sized army from such small beginnings. Before I move on to

Britain's world position was based on the Royal Navy and her Empire. There seemed little need for a large army.

the main sections of my little book, several explanatory notes need to be made. The first of these is the use of the term 'British'. That word can be vague. It can be applied just to the United Kingdom (England, Scotland, Wales and the whole of Ireland in 1914) or it can be used to describe the wider contribution in the war of the British Empire. For the purposes of this book I have decided that the terms 'Britain' and 'British' will apply only to units from those four home countries which made up the United Kingdom in 1914. The Empire countries, particularly the white dominions, achieved similar heroic effort of military expansion and contribution to the war, but my work will cover only the 'home' British effort.

The Infantry Division

The war would mainly be an infantry and artillery war. The British Army had a cavalry arm but the pre-war cavalry units sent to the Western Front saw little action in the mounted role and there would be no need for any major wartime expansion. The almost immediate transformation of the campaign into trench warfare would require the British Expeditionary Force – the BEF – to man an ever-growing mileage of those trenches and to build up further forces for attacks to break the trench stalemate. There would also be the need to provide

Soldier contingent aboard His Majesty's warship – the Royal Marines. Here a platoon, armed with Lee-Metfords, undergoes rifle inspection.

expeditionary forces for other theatres of war. My *From Six to Sixty-Five* talk and this book concern themselves exclusively with infantry divisions.

Infantry divisions of 1914 varied in size between approximately 15,000 men – a French division, through 17,500 – a German division, to nearly 20,000 for the British. For that British division which went to war I have found three sets of figures, all claiming to be based on the official war establishment, but varying in strength between 18,073 and 19,630. The most interesting set of figures are those I found in *War Establishments for 1907-1908* (bought for £5 in a secondhand book shop). A large sheet contained a table showing every officer, every other rank, every gun, vehicle and horse, for the whole of the Expeditionary Force of six infantry divisions and one cavalry division envisaged at that time and which, with little change, actually went to France in 1914.

The basic British infantry division comprised three infantry brigades of four battalions each, four artillery brigades (much smaller than infantry brigades) and a heavy artillery battery, together with supporting units. French and German divisions were organized differently, but contained much the same proportion of infantry, artillery, etc. The 1907-1908 establishment shows the following breakdown of the British division's manpower:

The sovereignty of Belgium was violated when the German armies swept over that nation's borders, 4 August 1914. Men of the the 47th Infantry Regiment in the opening days of the war.

Divisional Headquarters	71
Infantry	12,132
Artillery	4,449
Service Corps	1,394
Medical Corps	702
Engineers	493
Cavalry (an attached squadron)	320
Military Police	25
Ordnance Corps	17
Postal Service	16
Veterinary Service	11

It is known that the attached cavalry strength was halved by 1914 and replaced by a cyclist company; this was the only major change. The division had five general officers: a major-general commanding the division, four brigadier-generals (three commanding the infantry brigades, one the divisional artillery), together with fourteen qualified staff officers and 579 regimental officers.

The establishment of the infantry division would increase during the first years of the war. Although the heavy artillery battery, with its four 60-pounders and 239 Royal Garrison Artillery gunners, was withdrawn to be placed under the control of the next higher formation – the army

Crowd outside Buckingham Palace awaiting Britain's declaration of war in August 1914.

German troops cautiously approaching a Belgian fort devastated by heavy siege artillery prior to an attack.

corps, there would be added a thirteenth infantry battalion to act as the division's pioneers, as well as specialist machine-gun and trench-mortar units to increase the infantry's firepower. The division would thus reach a strength of nearly 20,000 men at its peak in 1916, but would often be well below that figure once committed to battle. It would always be the infantry who bore the brunt of the casualties and the shortage would be so severe in early 1918 that a quarter of all the brigade infantry battalions would be disbanded, leaving the standard division with the three-battalion brigade which would fight the Second World War.

So this story will concern itself with a standard infantry division up to 20,000 men strong, with three brigades, twelve infantry battalions, a pioneer battalion and its artillery and other supporting units.

The British Infantry Regiment

There remains one major element of our story which requires explanation. While the strength of the British infantry division did not vary greatly from that of the other armies of 1914, the means by which the infantry battalions were provided were not only quite unique but also of much interest.

In most armies a regiment is an active field formation, usually of what in the British Army would be of brigade strength. For British infantry, a regiment is quite different. It is the organization, on a regional basis, under which an unlimited number of battalions can be

The German Kaiser Wilhelm II intent on dominating Europe.   *Germans in possession of the Belgian town of Bruges August 1914.*

formed and maintained, with personnel being recruited, trained, and supplied to those battalions. (The battalion is the standard small-scale infantry unit of most armies; in the British Army of 1914 it had an establishment of twenty-nine officers and 995 other ranks, all commanded by a lieutenant-colonel.)

What may loosely be called the County Regiment System was established by Edward Cardwell, Gladstone's Secretary of State for War, in 1881. Cardwell reduced the number of Foot regiments from 108 to sixty-seven and linked them more firmly to counties and areas. Each new regiment was to contain two active service battalions, one serving at home, the other overseas. The term 'county regiment' only refers strictly to England; the regiments were of a more regional nature in the less populated areas of Scotland, Wales and Ireland. Cardwell thus established a system whereby a soldier enlisted in a regiment, often but not always his local one. Officers were commissioned into a regiment, not so often his local one; military families often had long-standing links with regiments away from their homes. The soldier normally remained with his regiment throughout his period of service but could be freely transferred between battalions in that regiment. If he was sent away on detached duty to another unit he could expect to be returned to his regiment in due course. The same conditions applied to an officer, unless he was fortunate enough to be promoted to full colonel, in which case he ceased to be part of his regiment but became

Initial successes of the invading armies in covering large areas of territory seemed to indicate that the Schlieffen Plan was working.

part of the General Staff and available for duty anywhere in the Army. Even if an officer had to be transferred to a battalion in another regiment because of a shortage there, he remained a member of his old regiment. An example of this can be seen in a cemetery some readers may have visited, the Fricourt New Cemetery where Lieutenant-Colonel A. Dickson, commanding the 10th West Yorkshires and killed with them in the opening attack of the Battle of the Somme in 1916, has a grave, among rows of headstones with the West Yorkshires' badge, but his bearing the badge of the South Lancashires, the regiment into which he had been commissioned as a young man many years earlier.

Before the Cardwell reforms, the British Army had consisted of three types of battalions, the Regulars – professional soldiers available for active service anywhere, the Militia and the Volunteers – part-time local units but of different types. Each had been an independent force. Cardwell had given the three a common bond when all became parts of one of the new regiments. There was a further reorganization in 1908 when a new Secretary of State for War, Lord Haldane, drew upon the experiences of the Boer War to make improvements in the county-regiment system. The professional Regulars remained largely unchanged. The Militia, originally a force drawn by compulsory ballot to provide reinforcements for the Regulars in time of war, now became the Special Reserve for which men could volunteer, receive six months' training and then remain in civilian life on part-pay but liable for recall

Belgian troops with dog teams pulling machine guns. The Belgian army was outdated and no match for the invaders. Manning a road block that was easily outflanked and swept aside.

in time of war. The old Volunteers became the new part-time Territorial Force (later the Territorial Army) with its members liable to be called to full-time service in time of war, but only committed to home defence duties.

The Haldane Reforms were well established by the outbreak of war in August 1914. Their effects can be seen in a typical county regiment, that of my home county, the Lincolnshire Regiment:

The Depot, at the New Barracks, Lincoln

1st (Regular) Battalion, in barracks at Portsmouth

2nd (Regular) Battalion, on garrison duty in Bermuda

3rd (Special Reserve) Battalion, New Barracks, Lincoln

4th (Territorial) Battalion, at Drill Halls in South Lincolnshire towns

5th (Territorial) Battalion, at Drill Halls in North Lincolnshire towns

(The Lincolns became the Royal Lincolns after the Second World War and the New Barracks at Lincoln became Sobraon Barracks in 1954.)

It was at the depot, commanded by a major, that a Regular recruit enlisted, was kitted out and received basic training. He signed on for seven years' full-time service, followed by five years on the Regular Army Reserve. These figures will have much significance later in our story.

An essential part of the current army organization was that the

French infantry moving forward to meet the German hordes swarming across French countryside and heading for Paris.

standard regiment should have one Regular battalion at home and one at an overseas station. A newly trained recruit was posted to the home battalion for about two years and then to the overseas battalion for the balance of his Regular service. These relative periods of service meant that the home battalion was always well below its war establishment strength, while the overseas one was kept as near up to strength as possible. It also meant that the home battalion was mostly composed of men with an average of only eighteen months or so of service experience, while the overseas battalion man had completed about five years of service. The importance of all this is that when war broke out in August 1914 the greater part of Britain's Regular Army and the most experienced members of it were at overseas stations, not in the units earmarked for the British Expeditionary Force.

The 3rd (Special Reserve) Battalion was only a skeleton unit in peacetime. Most of its members were in civilian life, having completed their six months of training. On the outbreak of war the permanent staff of the Depot and of the 3rd Battalion were almost one unit. Their task was to receive and process the recalled Regular Army Reservists and the Special Reservists. What happened then will be described later, but the important thing to remember is that the Special Reserve existed to

Opening moves of the Great War as presented to the public through the pages of **The Sphere** *magazine. It shows the sweep into France by the German armies, with the French capital under threat.*

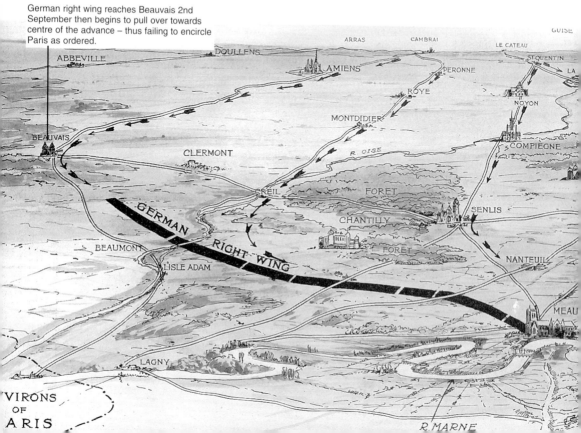

German right wing reaches Beauvais 2nd September then begins to pull over towards centre of the advance – thus failing to encircle Paris as ordered.

supply the Regular battalions with reinforcements, not the Territorials and not the New Army that Kitchener would soon be creating.

The number of Territorial battalions in a regiment varied according to the local population. The smallest counties only had one Territorial battalion; many rural counties like Lincolnshire had two; some of the industrial areas had up to six; London had a whole host. None of the eight Irish regiments had Territorial battalions, however; there had been no Volunteer battalions in Ireland for Haldane to turn into Territorials in his 1908 reforms. What happened to the Territorials on the outbreak of war will be a major part of our story.

Many English counties, because of their size, did not fit into the standard system. Small counties could not maintain two Regular battalions; large ones could provide many more. Some medium-sized counties – Kent, Surrey and Staffordshire – had two regiments, each with its complete Depot, Regular, Special Reserve and Territorial units. Large Yorkshire had six regiments; Lancashire had seven – the King's Own (Royal Lancaster), King's (Liverpool), Lancashire Fusiliers, East Lancashires, South Lancashires, Loyal North Lancashires and Manchesters. After the Cardwell reforms the newly formed regiments were given an order of seniority more or less following that of their old

Von Schlieffen's plan for the invasion of France called for the right wing of the attacking force to sweep around the north of Paris. In the event the German right wing, which had the most ground to cover, failed to follow the plan and pulled in towards the centre and there followed the Battle of the Marne.

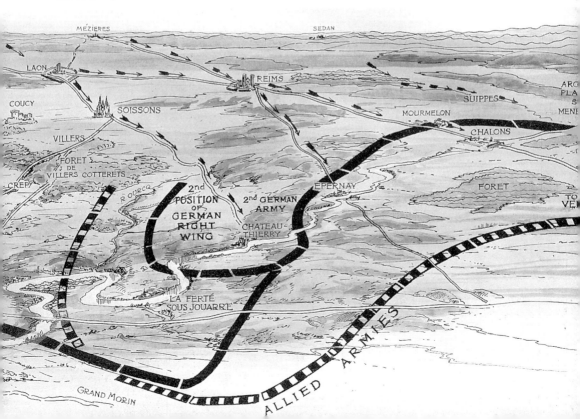

Foot Regiment predecessors. Thus in Lancashire, the senior regiment was the King's Own – the old 4th of Foot – while the most junior was the Manchesters – formed from the old 63rd and 96th of Foot. (If the reader visits any Memorial to the Missing of either World War, he or she will find the 'Infantry of the Line' shown in order of that seniority, with the Royal Scots, the old 1st of Foot – known as Pontius Pilate's Bodyguard – coming first, followed by the Queen's (Royal West Surreys) and the Buffs (East Kents), the old 2nd and 3rd of Foot. This leads to the saying 'Steady the Buffs', the full quotation being:

> 'Steady the Buffs,
> Halt the Queens,
> Let the Royals go by.'

– presumably some order given at a ceremonial parade long ago.

Coming back to departures from the normal county regiment, several English counties had such small populations that they could not support two Regular battalions but were allowed to have a Territorial one; Cambridgeshire, Herefordshire, Hertfordshire, Huntingdonshire and Monmouthshire all fell into this category. Their men who wished to become Regular soldiers had to go to a neighbouring county to enlist in a regiment to which their county was traditionally linked. Hertford and Huntingdon men both went to the Bedfords; Hereford men went to the King's Shropshire Light Infantry and Monmouths to the South Wales Borderers; Cambridge men went to Suffolk which is why, when Cambridge formed a battalion for Kitchener's New Army in 1914, it had to serve as the 11th Suffolks when it met its destiny on the first day of the Battle of the Somme in front of the Lochnagar Crater at La Boisselle. Other small counties were allowed to amalgamate, hence the Border Regiment for Cumberland and Westmorland, the Oxfordshire and Buckinghamshire Light Infantry, though why well populated Nottinghamshire and Derbyshire had to share one regiment between them in the Sherwood Foresters is not clear. Do not, however, let the York and Lancaster Regiment confuse you; it recruited exclusively in South Yorkshire.

Finally, in this survey of the English counties, there were three regiments which, after the 'Black Week' of three disasters in December 1899 in the Boer War, were each ordered to raise two extra Regular battalions, together with an extra Special Reserve battalion to support them. Three regiments with better than average recruiting records were chosen, the Royal Fusiliers (City of London), the Worcestershires and the Middlesex. These three regiments would thus enter the 1914 war with four Regular battalions each. (They would disband the extra two battalions when the British Army lost the need to provide a garrison in

Southern Ireland in the early 1920s.)

The Foot Guards – Grenadier, Coldstream, Scots and Irish only in 1914, not yet the Welsh, were not part of the county-regiment system and had only Regular battalions – no Special Reserve, no Territorials. The two Rifle regiments – the King's Royal Rifle Corps and the Rifle Brigade with their shared depot at Winchester – were not strictly speaking part of the county-regiment system, but they did have Special Reserve battalions. They also had excellent recruiting records and had been allowed to recruit two extra battalions each after that Boer War disaster week in 1899. The Territorial aspects of the two Rifle regiments were complicated. Both had strong links with London and recruited many of their Regulars there. Twelve London Volunteer battalions had been part of the King's Royal Rifle Corps and the Rifle Brigade – six each – up to the Haldane Reforms of 1908 and their successor Territorial battalions would officially return to them in 1916, but they were not officially linked in 1914. The Territorial situation of another Regular regiment, the Royal Fusiliers, throws up another anomaly. This regiment's secondary title was 'The City of London'; it recruited in the traditional financial City. But its pre-war Territorial battalions formed part of the all-Territorial London Regiment. These are all typical of the ever-changing complexities of the British regimental system.

The full line-up of British Army Regular battalions serving at the outbreak of war in 1914 was:

Guards – 9 battalions (3 each Grenadier and Coldstream, 2 Scots, 1 Irish)

2 Rifle Regiments – 8 battalions

43 English County Regiments – 86 battalions

3 Double-Strength English County Regiments – 12 battalions

10 Scottish Regiments – 20 battalions

8 Irish Regiments -16 battalions

3 Welsh Regiments – 6 battalions

Total – 157 battalions

Of these, the Guards and seventy-five understrength battalions were stationed in various parts of Britain, with the remaining seventy-three battalions, at full strength, serving abroad from as near as a battalion in Guernsey to as far as three in China. Approximately half of the overseas battalions were in India.

The county-regiment system may have had disadvantages but these were easily outweighed by its benefits. Men who are good soldiers fight well for their self-esteem, for the sake of their comrades and for their country. British soldiers usually fight that bit better for the honour of their regiment. The system also allowed the disparate elements in the nation to preserve their identity while still being efficient members of one army. A British brigade could go to war in 1914 with battalions from, say, the Wiltshires, the Royal Welsh Fusiliers, the Gordon Highlanders and the Royal Irish Rifles. They might have argued when out of the line but they would never have let each other down in battle. The two world wars saw the glory days of the county-regiment system. I often look around a cemetery in France or Belgium or at Gallipoli and love to see all the regimental badges on the headstones, though the Southern Irish regiments are absent in the 1939-45 cemeteries. 'That,' I tell my battlefield-touring customers, 'was the British Army that fought and won the two World Wars and it was also the army in which I did my humble National Service in the early 1950s.' But most of it has gone now. It is history.

The county-regiment system of the British army engendered self-esteem, and usually it meant that an individual would fight that bit better for the honour of his regiment. This is a squad of recruits of the Duke of Cornwall's Light Infantry prior to the outbreak of war.

CHAPTER ONE

The Regular Divisions

Mobilization

An army mobilizes when it recalls its reserves and places its military units on a war footing. Mobilization plans were always carefully prepared and kept up to date, but it was a process that was complicated, expensive, not to be undertaken lightly and not easily reversed if found to have been unnecessary.

The assassination of the Austrian Archduke by a Bosnian Serb nationalist on 28 June 1914 was the spark which caused the European powers, in turn, to invoke treaties and call for help from allies – always willingly given, make demands on potential opponents – always defied, and then tumble into a world war. Austria, Russia, Germany, France and, finally Britain all carried out this process and issued mobilization orders within a five-day period, Britain's decision being made at 4.00 pm on 4 August, seven hours before the declaration of war on Germany.

The means by which the British reserves were recalled was usually that of the police placing a notice in the local Post Office. Word soon spread and the thousands of former soldiers serving their period of seven years' reserve commitment made their way to the depots of the

One of the results of mobilization in this country: ammunition being brought out of store at Hyde Park in requisitioned carts. The ammunition was delivered to London Bridge Station and from there distributed to various centres throughout the land.

units in which they had once served. Although most of the following description refers to infantry, the same process was being experienced by artillery, cavalry and the other arms, as well as by the Royal Navy.

The British plans worked smoothly. Uniforms and equipment were issued, often being the same items that men had handed in on completion of their Regular service. Medical tests were carried out. Within two days the depots were sending drafts off to bring their home-based units up to war establishment. The records of the Royal Norfolks (just the Norfolks in 1914) give a typical experience. Approximately 800 Reservists reported for duty at Britannia Barracks, Norwich. On 6 August, 700 were sent to the 1st Battalion then serving at Hollywood Barracks, Belfast, and two days later Lieutenant-Colonel C.R. Ballard could report that his battalion was fully up to war establishment in all respects. A 'Base Party' of 100 men was also complete; these would be the 'first reinforcements' eventually sent to the infantry base in France. A total of 132 men – mostly new recruits in the pre-war battalion and Reservists found to be medically unfit – would be left behind at Hollywood and 109 surplus Reservists were returned to Norwich.

That figure of 109 spare Reservists is an important one; it shows that most of the men of the Regular Army Reserve were required to bring the home-based units up to full strength, leaving little as a further reserve for eventualities.

Before leaving for the Continent the 2nd Battalion Grenadier Guards marched past Buckingham Palace in full marching order. King George V can be seen doffing his hat in salute.

THE BRITISH EXPEDITIONARY FORCE

The first four divisions of the BEF were ready to start crossing to France on 12 August and were concentrated there by the 17th, a triumph for the creators of the Mobilization Plan and the work of the units and their regimental depots. They would be fighting their first battle at Mons eleven days later. The last two divisions followed more leisurely, with the 6th Division from locations mainly in Ireland completing the assembly of the BEF in France on 13 September.

Those first six divisions start the telling of our *From Six to Sixty-Five* story:

1st Division

Stationed in the Aldershot area on the outbreak of war, with two Guards battalions and ten other battalions. Crossed to France on 11-15 August 1914 and fought its first battle at Mons. The division remained on the Western Front until the Armistice in 1918, taking part in most of the major battles.

2nd Division

Stationed mainly at Aldershot, but with the 4th (Guards) Brigade in London and Windsor. Crossed to France on 11-15 August and fought at Mons. Served on the Western Front until the Armistice.

British Regulars leaving England to join the French and Belgian armies already engaging the Germans.   *The Black Watch (1st Battalion) marching across the harbour bridge, Boulogne, 14 August 1914.*

3rd Division

Its pre-war stations were in Southern Command. Crossed to France on 11-16 August and fought at Mons. Served on the Western Front until the Armistice.

4th Division

Its pre-war stations were in Eastern Command. Crossed to France on 22 August. Took part in the Retreat from Mons; its first battle was Le Cateau. Served on the Western Front until the Armistice.

5th Division

Its pre-war stations were in Ireland. Crossed from Ireland to France, completing the move on 17 August, and fought at Mons. Served on the Western Front until the Armistice, except for the period November 1917 to March 1918 when it was transferred to the Italian Front.

6th Division

Pre-war stations: 16th and 17th Brigades in Ireland, 18th Brigade in Northern Command. The division concentrated in England and started crossing to France on 9 September. Its first battle was the Aisne later in September. Served on the Western Front until the Armistice.

The British Expeditionary Force was complete in every way. Here a section of the Army Signals Service, Royal Engineers, poses for a photograph in the main square at Merville.

Because these first divisions were fully assembled and went straight to war and because they remained on the Western Front, with the one temporary absence in Italy of the 5th Division, their descriptions above will appear short and possibly uninteresting in comparison to those of later divisions which had more varied origins and war experiences.

It cannot be stressed too strongly, however, that these first six Regular divisions, and most of those Regulars who followed as soon as they could be recalled from their overseas stations, fought in nearly every battle of the Western Front and suffered casualties accordingly. The average Regular battalion, which went to war 1,000 strong, would have about 1,500 men killed and 3,000 sick and wounded during the next four years. The chances of an original soldier in a rifle company surviving unhurt were almost non-existent.

It should also be stressed that these divisions suffered frequent changes, with battalions being transferred between divisions for various reasons. As far as is known, all of the original Regular battalions survived the war, but they would be widely spread between divisions by the war's end.

There had been no holding back by the British Government. The planned BEF was complete in every way. Its strength was approximately 166,300 men and 786 female nursing staff. Of the eighty-four infantry battalions available in Britain, seventy-two were in the six BEF divisions, five more were allocated to the BEF's Lines of

British cavalry passing through the Grande Place, Ypres, in the late summer of 1914. As yet the Germans have not begun their artillery bombardment that would eventually reduce the fine buildings to rubble.

Communication (four of them would soon be formed into a spare infantry brigade) and one more battalion, the 1st Queen's Own Cameron Highlanders, was a spare battalion in the BEF. That left only six Regular battalions in the whole of Great Britain. The infantry element of the six BEF infantry divisions totalled 117,718 men. To this can be added 11,724 infantry 'details' at the BEF's base camp, most of these being the 'first reinforcements' to replace the infantry units' first 10 per cent casualties. The total infantry was thus 129,504 – 78 per cent of the BEF's manpower. Most of the remainder were the 31,463 artillerymen and the 6,400 cavalrymen; the cavalrymen would soon be fighting valiantly as dismounted infantry in the desperate days of the First Battle of Ypres in October.

History acknowledges that the original BEF was a superb force, every man fully trained, well equipped and supported by modern artillery. Its efficiency was based on that long, seven-year term of Regular or 'active' service, compared to the conscript German soldier's two-years service when called up at age twenty (three years for cavalry and horse artillery), and the Frenchman's three years' active conscript service. But Britain was embarking on a continental war among armies based on universal male conscription. It is little wonder that a German is supposed to have called the BEF 'a contemptible little army'. The 'contemptible' referred to the BEF's size, not its quality. When Britain sent its six infantry divisions to France in those early days of the war,

Infantry being bused up to the front to meet the German hordes. Cavalry riding through a Belgian village during the early days of a war of movement.

France had already mobilized sixty-one divisions and the Germans 110 divisions, of which seventy-eight would soon be facing the British and French on the Western Front. Not only that, but the French and Germans had only recalled the younger of their reserve classes. As the war progressed, they would be steadily calling in the older classes of reserve. Britain, by comparison, had dispatched almost all of its home-based Regular units, and had recalled and already employed most of its reserves. The hard fighting that ensued almost at once rapidly drew in the 10 per cent first reinforcements at the base camps in France and then the remainder of the Reservists at home. So dire became the need for men that Territorial battalions, half-trained and intended for home defence, had to be rushed out to France in November and were attached to the BEF's infantry divisions in place of normal reinforcements.

The Overseas Garrisons Come Home

Several dramatic moves by the British Government were being made to remedy that shortage of men. Britain was determined not only to maintain the strength of the BEF but to expand it; her resolve to play the major-power role was undiminished. The first of those moves involved the recall from the overseas stations of most of that part of the Army that was protecting vulnerable parts of the Empire.

There were seventy-three infantry battalions at various locations

Bringing up the guns in the early stages of the war. Compared to the conscripted German army the small British Expeditionary Force taking the field did indeed appear 'contemptible'.

abroad. The risk was taken to strip as many as possible of these places of their garrisons and bring the battalions home as quickly as shipping could be provided. Twenty-nine battalions came home from India and a further six British battalions would be in the Indian divisions which went directly to France. Other battalions withdrawn were: from Egypt and Malta five battalions each, South Africa four, Burma and China three each, Gibraltar two, and Aden, Bermuda, Guernsey, Hong Kong and Mauritius one each. To replace some of these withdrawals, partly trained Territorials were sent to India and to Gibraltar, Malta, Egypt and Aden to protect the vital Mediterranean and Suez Canal route to India and the Far East. (There would still be 93,670 British troops in India and Burma at the end of the war, and another 12,497 at other minor stations, the equivalent of five divisions.)

At battalion level the returning units needed little reorganization to be ready for service in France. They were almost at full war establishment strength. The potential efficiency of these units was the highest of the whole British Army. Whereas the home-based battalions which formed the original BEF were composed of approximately 40 per cent young soldiers, with an average of no more than two years of service, and 60 per cent Reservists who had been enjoying the softer life of civilians, the men in the battalions from overseas were all mature Regulars with an average of five years' recent hard service. Any time-expired men among them were immediately re-engaged, it being deemed that they were now recalled Reservists. A short home leave was

Sir John French, BEF Commander in Chief.

Men of 1st Battalion, the Leicestershire Regiment on their way to the front.

allowed. The few medically unfit were replaced by men from the regimental depots.

It was decided to use these battalions, not to replace casualties being suffered by the BEF, but to form new Regular divisions. But no divisional framework existed into which the battalions could be fitted. Some of the artillery and engineer units and other arms were provided by spare Regular units in England or others withdrawn from overseas, but many had to be hurriedly raised from Reservists or wartime volunteers and their equipment provided from stores which soon ran short. Divisional and brigade commanders and their staffs had to be found. This was the start of a long and not always satisfactory search for such officers for new divisions; but these new Regular divisions fared better in this respect than later creations.

7th Division

Formed in the New Forest area between 31 August and 4 October 1914 from three of the Regular battalions still remaining in England and nine from relatively near overseas stations. Landed at Zeebrugge and Ostend on 6 and 7 October to become part of an independent force with the 3rd Cavalry Division landing at Ostend and the Royal Naval Division at Antwerp, in an attempt to save Antwerp from German capture. Despite much marching and countermarching, the 7th Division could not reach Antwerp and provide help there but moved south to join the BEF on 14 October, becoming the first British unit to

British regulars of a Scottish regiment crossing a canal in Belgium on their way to meet the invaders.

take part in the defence of Ypres.

The division remained on the Western Front until November 1917 when it was transferred to Italy until the Armistice.

8th Division

Formed in Hampshire in October 1914 with battalions from India, Egypt, Malta, Aden and South Africa. Joined the BEF on 6 and 7 November 1914. The division's first major battle was Neuve Chapelle. It served on the Western Front until the Armistice.

(In a process to be described later, six of these first eight Regular divisions would each be forced to exchange a brigade or several battalions with a later wartime-raised division. Only the 1st and 4th Divisions would remain totally Regular in composition to the end. The replacement of heavy casualties over the next four years would, however, steadily reduce the Regular-soldier element in all of these early divisions, almost to nothing in their infantry units, but the ethos of the old Regular Army would persist in some degree.)

The Last of the Old Army

The battalions returning from the more distant stations arrived in England several weeks after divisional numbers 9th to 26th were allocated to what would be known as Kitchener's New Army. There had been an earlier plan to use these last Regular battalions as 'training

Preparing a defensive line to try and hold back the hordes of German infantry streaming through Belium.

Firing on the advancing massed ranks.

cadres' for the New Army, to provide war-time raised units with a framework of experienced officers and men, but the desperate fighting of the First Battle of Ypres in October and November 1914 persuaded the War Office to form three more divisions, the last of the Regular Army.

27th Division

Formed in the Winchester area in November and December 1914 with ten battalions from India and one each from Hong Kong and Tientsin in China. Unusually, a thirteenth battalion was added, the Princess Patricia's Canadian Light Infantry, which had just been formed in Canada from former British Army Regulars who had emigrated. This unit wished to serve, not with the Canadian Expeditionary Force then being formed, but with the British Army, so was added to the 27th Division.

The division crossed to France just before Christmas 1914. In April and May 1915 it was heavily involved in the Second Battle of Ypres, facing German attacks on the Frezenberg Ridge and suffering severe casualties, but being credited with having contributed substantially to saving the front at Ypres. The division, in weakened condition, remained on the Western Front only until November 1915 when it left to serve the remainder of the war, with four other British divisions, on the Salonika Front in Greece, in a confusing and doubtfully justified

German troops advancing towards Ypres. Many of them were students who volunteered on the outbreak of war and were sent into the fray with little training.

diversion of effort in the Balkans. The division's casualties at Salonika were, however, much lower than if it had continued on the Western Front.

The Princess Patricia's Canadian Light Infantry left when the division went to Salonika and it served the remainder of the war with the Canadians.

28th Division

Formed in the Winchester area in December 1914 and January 1915 with ten battalions from India and one each from Egypt and Singapore. It followed the 27th Division to the Western Front and had identical experiences to that division, also finishing up at Salonika in early 1916. The 27th and 28th Divisions are two of the almost 'forgotten' divisions of the war, but their self-sacrifice in the Second Battle of Ypres should not be forgotten. *The British Official History* (1915 Volume I, page 310) describes their action in that battle as 'some of the most desperate fighting that ever took place on the Ypres Salient'.

After the Armistice with Turkey in November 1918, the 28th Division was sent to reoccupy the old Gallipoli Peninsula battlefields, with headquarters at Chanak (now the modern Canakkale where my partner and I base our touring groups when visiting Gallipoli). The division, much changed in organization from its original form, remained in Turkey for some time, becoming involved in semi-active

Rows of German dead, ranks of men cut down by rifle fire. The British Regular Army prided itself on the ability of its infantry to loose off a regular flow of aimed shots.

operations when Britain's former ally, Greece, invaded. The last elements of the division departed from Constantinople (now Istanbul) in October 1923, giving the 28th Division the distinction of having the longest operational record of all First World War divisions.

29th Division

Formed in the Midlands in early 1915 with the last eleven battalions to return home, all from the Far East. An Edinburgh Territorial battalion, the 1/5th Royal Scots, completed the infantry composition. The division – the veritable last of Britain's Regular Army – was reluctantly allocated to the Mediterranean Expeditionary Force on the understanding that it was to be transferred to the Western Front as soon as the proposed Gallipoli campaign could be concluded.

There is a fine memorial where the division paraded along the main road from Daventry to Coventry (now the A45) before embarkation. The memorial is inscribed with all of the original units in the division and now stands in the centre of a roundabout at the junction of that road and the Fosse Way, near the village of Stretton-on-Dunsmore.

The division took part in the opposed landings on the Helles beaches at Gallipoli on 25 April 1915 and was present until the last evacuations in February 1916; it was the only Regular division in that campaign. Transferring to the Western Front in March 1916, it took part in the opening of the Battle of the Somme on 1 July 1916. Before leaving

By the end of 1914 the war of movement was over and the scene was set for the next four years as both sides dug in and trench warfare began.

Gallipoli, the Edinburgh Territorial battalion had fallen so far below strength that it had to be withdrawn. It was replaced by the volunteer 1st Newfoundland Regiment which, Newfoundland not then being part of Canada, also wished to serve in the British Army, not with the Canadians. So it was in the illustrious company of the 29th Division that the Newfoundlanders took part in the opening day of the Battle of the Somme, suffering (with one other battalion) the heaviest casualties of that day. This is why the 29th Division Western Front Memorial finds itself in what is now The Newfoundland Memorial Park at Beaumont Hamel.

The 29th Division served on the Western Front for the remainder of the war.

There were two further divisions which can usefully be included here.

The Guards Division

Nine battalions of Foot Guards had been present in Britain on the outbreak of war. Six had gone straight to France with the original BEF; two more followed with the 7th Division.

The Grenadier, Coldstream and Irish Guards each formed a new wartime battalion and opportunity was also taken to create for the first time a battalion of Welsh Guards from men with Welsh connections serving in the other four Guards regiments. Together with the last pre-

British prisoners captured in the early battles of mobility, seen here working in Germany helping with the harvest, 24 September 1914.

war Guards battalion still in England – the 3rd Grenadier – this made thirteen Guards battalions available, the number of battalions required for one division (an extra battalion having recently been added as pioneers to all divisions on the Western Front). It was decided to assemble all of these Guards battalions to create their own division which duly formed near St Omer in August 1915. The Guards battalions withdrawn from other divisions were replaced by other battalions, mostly of the New Army, a further dilution of those Regular divisions.

The Guards Division's first major action was in the Battle of Loos. It served on the Western Front until the Armistice, although one brigade would be transferred to another division in a major reorganization that would take place in early 1918.

The Royal Naval Division

When war appeared imminent in 1914, the Admiralty realized that it had many thousands of Reservists liable to recall for whom places could not be found in ships. On the outbreak of war these were formed into a division of three brigades, each of four battalions to conform with the organization of an Army division. (The Navy found itself between 2,000 and 2,500 men short for the division at various times in 1914, a shortage which led to an unusual link between the division and certain mining communities in the North of England. The local regiments of these had been hard-pressed to find accommodation for all of the many

Royal Marines arrive in Antwerp.

Men of the Royal Marines filling their water bottles at Ostend, August 1914.

recruits who rushed to join up in August and September 1914 and the War Office transferred some of them to accommodation that was available in the South. Documentary evidence of exactly what happened next is scarce, but it seems that the Army then forcibly transferred some of these men by discharging them and the Navy immediately re-engaging them on naval terms of service; others were sent directly to the division from the North by the same means. The men were, with very approximate numbers, 400 from the King's Own Yorkshire Light Infantry and the York and Lancasters, 400 from the Sherwood Foresters, and possibly 1,500 from the Northumberland Fusiliers and the Durham Light Infantry. Not only were these men assimilated into the Naval Division but their presence there in such large numbers encouraged friends and relatives in the North to volunteer for the Naval Division in subsequent months.)

The division took part in the failed Antwerp expedition in October 1914 and lost the service of 1,500 men who were cut off but who escaped to Holland where they were interned for the duration of the war. The division was sent to the Mediterranean in 1915 and served throughout the Gallipoli campaign, sustaining further heavy losses. In 1916 it was transferred to the Western Front and came under full Army control. One naval brigade was disbanded to bring the other two brigades up to strength, and four Army battalions joined the division to become the third brigade. At the same time the division was numbered 63rd, an earlier Army division of that number having been recently

Royal Marine Light Infantry of the Royal Naval Division 'on the Continent' according to the press caption; they are believed to be taking part in the failed Antwerp expedition in 1914.

disbanded, and became the 63rd (Royal Naval) Division. Its first Western Front battle was in the closing stages of the Battle of the Somme when it took most of its objectives in a major 'push' on 13 November 1916 and captured the village of Beaucourt-sur-Ancre where its main divisional memorial now stands, though it refers only to 'The Royal Naval Division', the Army's unpopular '63rd' part of its title having been deliberately omitted from the inscription.

The division served on the Western Front until the Armistice. Its casualties during the war numbered 47,953 killed, wounded and missing, equivalent to a total manpower turnover of two and a half times; the infantry turnover would have been much greater.

This concludes the listing of the first thirteen of our sixty-five fighting divisions.

Men of the Royal Naval Division in a 'rest camp' somewhere on the Helles sector during the Gallipoli campaign.

CHAPTER TWO

The New Army

It was the vigorous actions of one man that led to the British Army becoming so heavily involved in a war in which Britain was not directly threatened.

Field Marshal Earl Kitchener was appointed to be the new Secretary of State for War on the second day of the war. Prime Minister Asquith would have probably preferred to bring back Haldane who had made such a good job of the Army reforms six years earlier. Haldane was Lord Chancellor in August 1914, but he was unpopular because of his pro-German views. He had been partly educated in Germany which he had once described as 'his spiritual home' and had recently undertaken a secret mission to Germany in an attempt to improve relations between the two countries. These were the factors that prevented the re-appointment of the politician, Haldane, as Secretary of State for War, rather than the military man, Kitchener. It was a fateful decision. If Haldane had been acceptable it is almost certain that Britain would not have become involved as deeply as she eventually did under Kitchener's policy. Her casualties would have been lower, but the progress and the outcome of the war under a Haldane policy is impossible to judge.

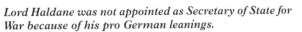

Field Marshal Earl Kitchener was appointed Secretary of State for War.

Lord Haldane was not appointed as Secretary of State for War because of his pro German leanings.

The euphoria that said 'all over by Christmas' is well known, so too is Kitchener's almost lone voice saying that it would become a world war and would last three years at least. Even that astounding estimate was well short of the eventual outcome. Kitchener moved with amazing speed and the Government acceded to his every request. Within twenty-four hours of the Declaration of War at 11.00 pm on 4 August, Kitchener stated that he wanted the Army to expand to a strength of seventy divisions and, on the following day, the first day of his actual appointment, the House of Commons sanctioned an increase in strength of half a million men, thus doubling the size of the Army at a stroke – and this would just be the beginning. Two days later posters and newspaper notices appeared appealing for the first stage of this increase, the famous 'First Hundred Thousand'. Men aged nineteen to thirty were asked to enlist for three years or the duration of the war. The words 'for three years or the duration of the war' caused some confusion. What if the war only lasted one or two years; would the men be released or retained for three years? I am not aware that this was ever clarified. In the end, the four-year period of the war resolved any doubts.

What was particularly radical about Kitchener's recruiting scheme was that these men were to be enlisted directly into the Regular Army, bypassing the Territorial Force for which Kitchener had no liking because it was not directly under War Office control but of that of County Territorial Associations, although the Haldane reforms had

Lord Kitchener delivering an address to the crowds and urging the young men to join for the duration of the war. He believed that it would last three years.

envisaged that it would be through the Territorials that any increase in Army strength in time of war would be made. The first 100,000 men would be formed into six completely new divisions, the forerunners of thirty new divisions for which Kitchener hoped further volunteers would come forward. Such optimism! Seventy divisions! Out of what? Six divisions of Regulars gone to war and a few more to be found by denuding the overseas garrisons. That left just fourteen Territorial divisions, understrength, only partially trained and intended for home defence. Where would the framework for the new divisions come from – the commanders, the staffs, the junior officers and the non-commissioned officers? Not from the old pre-war Army; the depots were almost bare. There were plenty of critics of Kitchener's high-handed actions. Commanders in France would soon be calling out that these new men would be best employed replacing the BEF's staggering early losses.

The story of how the volunteers flooded in has been told many times – nearly 300,000 men in that first month of August; 1,186,357 by the end of the year; another million and a quarter in 1915. But there are several features that should be stressed. The first is that the initial enlistments were carried out by the Army's own recruiting service, at the depots and the regular recruiting offices, or at hastily opened temporary offices; the stories of units raised by private initiative come later. Second, although this account concentrates heavily on infantry units, many thousands of men were also volunteering for the artillery,

Kitchener inspecting the guard of honour at the Guildhall. The recruiting posters on the walls call for 300,000 men.

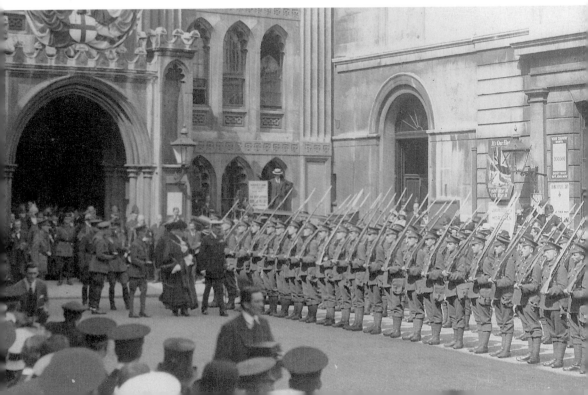

cavalry etc. Third, men could apply for a particular regiment and assume that their enlistment would guarantee service in that regiment. Once in a regiment, however, the man had no choice as to which battalion he was eventually sent. Some men who volunteered for the New Army would be sent as reinforcements to Regular battalions on the Western Front when all the Reservists were gone and be in action early in 1915, months before any New Army unit. The BEF needed to replace almost 20,000 casualties a month in 1914 and, from early 1915, these reinforcements could only come from returned wounded and wartime volunteers. Finally, although I have no statistics to prove this, I have always had the feeling that men from the industrial areas of England volunteered in higher proportions than other areas, witness the 2,000 surplus men from North Country regiments transferred to the Royal Naval Division in September 1914. It was probably escapism to fresh air and adventure from the drudgery of mine and factory work as much as patriotism which provided the motive in those areas.

The First Battalions Form

The first batch of seventy-two new battalions of infantry started to form. There were more than enough men, but acute shortages of everything else. Those first seventy-two battalions would require that number of battalion commanders and of adjutants, 288 company commanders and more than 1,500 junior officers; other divisional units would require half of those numbers. And Kitchener planned to repeat

Recruits signing on for the duration in London.

that process four more times! When the Regular battalions went to France, only a handful of officers were left at regimental depots. The Army had 2,500 Special Reserve officers and 3,000 of the younger retired officers liable for recall. Those who were not sent to the BEF to replace casualties provided the officer framework for the new units. Kitchener also found that there were more than 500 Regular officers home on leave from India; these were told not to return to India but were promptly posted to the new units. These early battalions were lucky; most would be provided with a battalion commander, an adjutant and up to four company commanders with some military experience. The situation in the later-formed units could only deteriorate.

To satisfy the need for junior officers, the War Office was able to draw on one of Haldane's innovations of 1908. Public schools and universities had been encouraged to provide Officer Training Corps at Army expense. There were twenty-three of these OTCs at universities and 166 at public schools. The War Office had records of all 'young gentlemen' who had completed such training. Letters were sent to the first 2,000 names on the list inviting them to apply for temporary commissions. The OTCs eventually provided 20,577 second lieutenants for Kitchener's expanding army. Battalion commanders were also allowed to recommend further suitable 'young gentlemen' for commissions. A total of 120,000 second lieutenants were created by direct commissioning before the practice ceased in February 1916 to be

Men of Kitchener's New Army leaving Whitehall with a brass band leading the way.

Public school Officer Training Corps provided the needed officers.

replaced by proper officer training units. Most of the 1914 and 1915 commissioned junior officers joined their units without military training of any kind, but 6,713 would be valuable material commissioned from the ranks.

The shortage of non-commissioned officers was just as acute. A few Regulars from the depots or spare Reservists were quickly promoted and were worth their weight in gold. Old soldiers out of their Reserve time were allowed to re-enlist even if over thirty years of age and many a veteran who had never earned a lance-corporal's stripe in seven years of service suddenly found himself promoted. Colonel A.P.B. Irwin, who helped me with *The First Day on the Somme*, describes his experience when the 8th East Surreys was formed in the second round of New Army divisions.

'I was a junior lieutenant in the Regular Army and was sent to be adjutant of a new battalion, the 8th East Surreys. I stood in the station yard at Purfleet and waited for the men to arrive. All I had for battalion headquarters was in my haversack. Three trains arrived during the day, bringing 1,000 men who had been wished upon us before any attempt had been made to provide accommodation. We only had two elderly retired officers and a quartermaster, and a very good sergeant major was the only N.C.O. We were given a dozen old Reservists, whom we promptly made lance-corporals, much to their horror and indignation. Then the whole battalion was paraded and an appeal was made for anybody who had ever been in charge of

A mixture of various military and civilian dress is seen here among these members of the Royal Artillery parading at Plymouth.

anyone else, or who wanted to be. About forty men stepped forward; we tied white tape around their arms and made them lance-corporals too. A rough and ready system, but it worked out well and nearly all of them made good.'

Irwin, a lieutenant in 1914, was a lieutenant-colonel in command of the battalion by 1916.

The Divisions Form

Less than three weeks after the outbreak of war, on 23 August 1914, the framework of the first six New Army divisions was ready. These became known as the K1 divisions, or the First Kitchener Army. The term 'Army' is misleading here. They were never intended to become operational field armies; the K 'Armies' were simply five groupings of six divisions each to be created one after the other.

The War Office decided, probably to encourage recruiting and also for ease of organization, that the new divisions should have regional titles. The Army in Britain was organized into eight administrative areas – the Scottish, Irish, Northern, Eastern, Western, Southern and Aldershot Commands and the London District. Aldershot was heavily involved in dispatching the BEF and the London District was only a small organization. That left six large command headquarters and staffs able to help form the first six new divisions. The original plan was to form one each of those first six divisions in each command area. I am assuming that it was pressure from the Rifle and Light Infantry element

Preparing to feed in the field.

in the Army that a successor to the famous Light Divisions of Napoleonic and Crimean War days should somehow be found a place in the New Army. In this way any proposal that there should be a Southern Division was dropped and a Light Division substituted in this first group; moreover, the Light Division would be the senior of the new divisions.

Kitchener insisted that the New Army divisions should have priority of numbering over the fourteen Territorial divisions which had been in existence for several years but had not yet been allocated divisional numbers. The first table of the new divisions was thus:

> 8th (Light) Division
> 9th (Scottish) Division
> 10th (Irish) Division
> 11th (Northern) Division
> 12th (Eastern) Division
> 13th (Western) Division

Unfortunately for the Light Division, further battalions from overseas garrisons started to form a new Regular division at that time which became the 8th Division. The Light Division then lost its place at the top of the list and fell to the bottom to become the 14th (Light) Division. It was intended that this order of seniority would be repeated for as long as possible with the later K divisions.

The creation of a Light rather than a Southern Division led to complications. The Light Division drew its battalions, not just from the

New Army men of the Queen's Regiment marching off to join the British Expeditionary Force in France.

Field Marshal Sir John French with his staff in France.

King's Royal Rifle Corps and the Rifle Brigade, but from Light Infantry regiments from as far apart as Cornwall and Durham. But the lack of a Southern Division left three county regiments on the South Coast – the Devonshires, Dorsetshires and Hampshires – without a New Army division to join. They became what I call 'orphan regiments'. Every other regiment, except one, in the whole of the United Kingdom found a home in the other new divisions. The exception was the Leicestershire Regiment. Leicestershire found itself bordered by counties whose regiments joined the Northern, Eastern and Western Divisions, but was not included in any of them. There were thus four regiments raising New Army battalions which became surplus to the new divisional organization and at the disposal of the War Office as spare units. Two early Devons battalions were sent to the 7th Division in France, replacing Guards battalions leaving to help form the new Guards Division. That is how the 8th and 9th Devons came to fight on the first day of the Battle of the Somme after which they buried their dead in their old front-line trench at Mansel Copse near Mametz, putting up a famous sign saying, THE DEVONSHIRES HELD THIS TRENCH, THE DEVONSHIRES HOLD IT STILL, this cemetery being now one of the most popular visiting places on the Somme battlefield. The Dorsets provided two battalions to fill a gap in each of the 11th and 17th (Northern) Divisions, the 5th Dorsets to go to Gallipoli and the 6th also to fight its first battle near Mametz on the Somme. The first two new Hampshire battalions were similarly sent to fill gaps in the

New battalion for the 'Tigers', the Leicestershire Regiment, taking a rest during a route march.

10th and 16th (Irish) Divisions, also to enter action respectively at Gallipoli and on the Somme. Four battalions of the Leicesters had to wait until April 1915 before being found a place in a later New Army division, also fighting their first battle on the Somme near Mametz; thereafter, all four Leicester battalions always served together in the same brigade.

There would be no problem about the supply of eager battalions for the new divisions, but the provision of divisional and brigade commanders and their staff officers presented great problems. By the time the first New Army divisions were ready to go overseas in the Spring of 1915, the Army had to find commanders and staffs for five new Regular divisions, eight army corps and two headquarters for the newly created level of command, 'army'. This expansion, together with the first three groups of Kitchener divisions, would require the following approximate numbers of experienced officers: 145 of general rank (two generals, eight lieutenant-generals, twenty-five major-generals and 110 brigadier-generals) and 364 staff officers.

The Army just did not have the required number of such officers. Some of the new divisions were fortunate and obtained excellent commanders, but the answer in many cases was the 'dug-out' officer. It is not meant to be a term of derision; the Official Histories quote it freely. The dug-outs were retired officers well past the normal age for active service. They were besieging the War Office in large numbers, begging to be employed. The War Office had no option but to fill the

General Headquarters staff hard at work.

gaping holes in the upper levels of the new divisions and brigades with these willing old warriors. Many would do well, but the age, health and out-of-touch notions of warfare of others would render them a liability under active service conditions and many would have to be replaced. All of this was a direct result of Kitchener's rush to create his large New Army. It often led to fine men being sent into battle by incompetent commanders and staff officers. The Germans, and the other Continental countries with conscript armies, had fewer problems; they had commanders and staffs in place at Reserve corps and divisional levels, ready to take in the Reserve fighting and support units on mobilization and lead them straight into action.

The K1 and K2 Divisions

The process of forming the new divisions proceeded rapidly. The first twelve were in existence within two months of the outbreak of war.

9th (Scottish) Division

Battalions were formed at Scottish regimental depots and the division assembled at Bordon in Hampshire on September 1914. It sailed for France between 9 and 12 May 1915, the first New Army division to proceed overseas. Its first battle was Loos, after which a reorganization of the division took place which will be described later. The division served on the Western Front until the Armistice, taking part in most of the major battles of 1916, 1917 and 1918, a comment

Royal Fusliers arrive in France. Some of the first of Kitchener's New Army to go overseas on active service.

that can apply to most of the New Army divisions which fought on the Western Front.

10th (Irish) Division

Initially composed entirely of Irish infantry, with the division forming in Ireland in August 1914, crossing to England in May 1915 and concentrating at Basingstoke. Sailed for the Mediterranean in July 1915 and, on 6 August, took part in the Suvla Bay landings at Gallipoli. Later served at Salonika and in Palestine, but the Irish battalions fell so low in strength that the division took in nine Indian battalions in 1918 to join the last three remaining Irish ones. The division lost its 'Irish' title at that time, but it continued to serve in Palestine until the end of the war.

(green)

11th (Northern) Division

Formed at Grantham in September 1914. Sailed for the Mediterranean in June and July 1915 and, with the 10th (Irish) Division, formed the Suvla Bay landing force at Gallipoli on 6 August 1915. Served at Gallipoli until the evacuation of Suvla in December. Transferred to the Western Front and served there from the Battle of the Somme in 1916 until the Armistice.

12th (Eastern) Division

The division assembled at Hythe, in Kent, in November 1914 and

Field Marshal Kitchener visits Gallipoli

crossed to France in June 1915. Its first battle was Loos. It then served on the Western Front until the Armistice.

13th (Western) Division

The division assembled on Salisbury Plain in August 1914 and sailed for the Mediterranean in June 1915. It fought in all three sectors of Gallipoli – Anzac, Suvla and Helles – and took part in two evacuations, from Suvla in December 1916 and from Helles the following month. The division served in Mesopotamia from April 1916 until the Armistice, with all of its original 'Western' infantry battalions present to the end, an almost unique record.

14th (Light) Division

Formed at Aldershot in September 1914 as the 8th (Light) Division but almost immediately became the 14th Division. The original battalions were three each from the King's Royal Rifle Corps and the Rifle Brigade and six battalions from English Light Infantry regiments, but none from the Highland Light Infantry which served with the Scottish divisions.

Crossed to France in May 1915. First action: the German 'Liquid-Fire' Attack at Hooge at the end of July in which 100 officers and 2,387 other ranks became casualties in two days of a vicious little engagement on the Ypres Salient. After the war, the divisional memorial in Belgium was erected at Railway Wood, close to where it fought that first action,

Transports land supplies on Anzac beach. Massed infantry rehearsing for an attack.

but it was later moved and now stands at the more accessible and much visited foot of Hill 60, just by the bridge over the railway.

The division served on the Western Front until after the German March Offensive in 1918 in which it suffered so heavily that its battalions were reduced to 'training cadres' and detached from the division. New battalions were posted in and made up to strength when the division, unusually, returned to England in June. The division went back to the Western Front in July 1918 and fought in the remaining battles of the war. None of the original battalions were present in this final stage, but two of the new battalions, the 10th Highland Light Infantry and 29th Durham Light Infantry, kept the original title of the division alive.

15th (Scottish) Division

Formed from Scottish regiments in September 1914 at Aldershot. Crossed to France in July 1915 in time to fight at Loos in September, when the division made a dramatic advance through Loos village and onto Hill 70 where it engaged in hand-to-hand fighting with the Germans. Like the 9th Division, however, the 15th suffered so heavily at Loos that it had to be reorganized. The division served on the Western Front until the Armistice.

16th (Irish) Division

Formed from Irish regiments in September 1914, with the divisional

An 18-pounder in action at Suvla Bay.

headquarters at Dublin and brigades at scattered locations in the south and west of Ireland. In 1915, three battalions which were short of recruits were made up with men from the Channel Islands Militias who had volunteered for overseas service. Guernsey sent company-sized contingents to the 6th Royal Irish and the 7th Royal Irish Fusiliers; Jersey provided a company for the 7th Royal Irish Rifles.

The division crossed to France in August and September 1915. Its first battle was on the Somme in September 1916 at Guillemont where the divisional memorial stands next to the village church. The division served on the Western Front until the Summer of 1918 when it became so weak in strength after the German March Offensive that, like the 14th Division, it had to return to England to be reconstituted. The end of the war found it back on the Western Front but the 5th Royal Irish Fusiliers, formerly in the 10th (Irish) Division, was the only Irish battalion left in the division.

It should be stated that the Irish soldiers in both the 10th and 16th Divisions always served loyally, with no open dissatisfaction over the delayed prospects for Home Rule, even after the 1916 Easter Rising in Dublin.

17th (Northern) Division

Formed in September 1914 at Wareham in Dorset. Crossed to France in July 1915. Involved in engagements at Hooge and the Bluff on the Ypres sector in August 1915 and early 1916. The first major

A truce is called at Anzac in order that the dead of both sides might be recovered and buried.

battle was at Fricourt on the Somme in July 1916. The division served on the Western Front until the Armistice.

18th (Eastern) Division

Formed around Colchester in September 1914. Crossed to France in July 1915. The division carried out several major attacks on the Somme in 1916, always being successful. Served on the Western Front until the Armistice, suffering more than 46,000 casualties, this high figure being the price of its successes in 1916 after which the division was called upon for attacks more often than those divisions judged to be no more than 'line-holders'.

19th (Western) Division

Formed in September 1914 at Bulford. Crossed to France in July 1915. The division played a diversionary role in the Battle of Loos; its first major battle was the capture of La Boisselle on the Somme in July 1916. Served on the Western Front until the Armistice.

20th (Light) Division

Formed in September 1914 at Aldershot, from the same Rifle and Light Infantry regiments as the 14th (Light) Division. Crossed to France in July 1915 and, after early engagements at Fromelles in September 1915 and on the Ypres Salient in June 1916, became heavily involved in the Battle of the Somme from fighting at Delville Wood in

Mounted troops moving through a Belgian town with an ambulance evacuating wounded to one of the Base Hospitals.

August onwards. Served on the Western Front until the Armistice.

So far, so good. Kitchener's plans seemed to be working well. Twelve new divisions had been formed in less than two months. But a shortage of men coming forward from two regions was beginning to cause strains on the regional aspects of the divisions.

The first of these areas was, surprisingly, the Eastern counties which would eventually produce three New Army divisions – 12th, 18th and 24th – with fine war records. Once the depots had sent off their Reservists to fill up their Regular battalions and the Special Reserve battalions went to their wartime stations protecting English ports, the depot staffs were not inundated with volunteers as in most other parts of the country. Taking Norfolk as an example, the first New Army battalion to form at Norwich, the 7th Norfolks, was slow in rising to full strength and local men only made up a little over half of that strength, the remainder being sent from other counties. Later in August, Kitchener expressed concern over this situation which was general throughout East Anglia; he sent a prominent politician, Ian Malcolm, who had earlier represented a Suffolk constituency, to make recruiting speeches right across the region. The press made daily exhortations throughout the month to local men. It was suggested that farmers, after the harvest, should sack single men who had not volunteered. Some patriot suggested that suitable men who had not joined should be shamed by making them wear petticoats! The problem was twofold.

Men of the Black Watch and Indians holding a sector of the line as trenches come into existence from the coast to the borders of Switzerland. Children used to put the pressure on.

One, the harvest. Wars should not start until the harvest is gathered in and this one had started prematurely. Farmers would find themselves shorthanded at the harvest from Sligo to Smolensk, but a particularly fine autumn would ensure that all would be safely gathered in as well as providing a long campaigning season. The second reason was the East Anglian nature – careful, preferring to think matters over before rushing into a venture. All came well in the end. By the end of September the harvest was safely completed and men came forward more willingly. The next two Norfolk battalions, the 8th and 9th, formed quickly, with three-quarters or so of their strength being local men, and the two Eastern divisions were completed on time.

A more enduring problem was appearing in Ireland. Many men in different sections of the population were reluctant to join and fight for Britain. Many Catholics were Nationalists, begrudging duty for a government that was delaying the complete introduction of Home Rule, even though public opinion throughout the Empire said they should have it. By contrast, Ulster had an armed and organized 'private army' – the Ulster Volunteer Force – made up of Protestants who were ready to fight any British move to force them into Home Rule with the Catholics. The UVF men were not prepared to join a division which also contained those same Catholics.

Voluntary recruitment was slow, jeopardizing Kitchener's plans to form two and possibly more Irish New Army divisions. The only overall figures available are for the period August 1914 to the end of 1915. Of

Irish troops at the front: The Royal Munster Fusiliers on Church Parade seen here on their way to attend Mass.

men between the ages of fifteen and forty-nine in mainland Britain, 24 per cent volunteered; in Ireland the figure was only 8 per cent. The 10th Division benefited from some English Catholics joining Irish regiments, and from Irishmen working on the mainland doing the same. But there are stories of officers with Ulster sympathies frustrating the normal recruiting process. An officer at the Royal Inniskilling Fusiliers depot at Omagh held back 400 men who had come in as unprejudiced volunteers and kept them for the Ulster Division which was soon to form. The War Office even sent letters to Inniskilling battalions already formed in the 10th and 16th Divisions, telling men who had volunteered earlier for those two divisions that permission would be given to them to transfer to the new Ulster Division if they wished to do so. Despite this shortage of volunteers, the commander of the 16th Division was unduly particular about the class of men who joined his division. When the Tyneside Irish community started to form battalions and suggested they serve in the division, he refused the offer.*

The general result was that most of the twenty-four Irish battalions in the 10th and 16th Divisions were short of recruits. Drafts from English regiments with surplus volunteers were sent across the Irish Sea to make up the shortages and we have seen how the Guernsey and Jersey contingents were used in the same way. When each division had to find a battalion to serve as the new divisional pioneer battalion, no

* I am indebted to Tom Johnstone, author of *Orange, Green and Khaki*, for these stories.

Men of the 26th Northumberland Fusiliers (3rd Tyneside Irish) on parade in the streets of Gateshead in 1915.

Irish regiment could be found with a spare battalion to fulfil that role. Two battalions from the Hampshires, one of the 'orphan' regiments left without a home in the English regional divisions, had to join the Irish, the 10th Hampshires to replace the 5th Royal Irish when that battalion become the 10th Division's pioneers and the 11th Hampshires becoming the pioneer battalion in the 16th Division.

The 10th Division would go to war with only 65-70 per cent of its infantrymen being Irish; the 16th Division did better and had 85 per cent but did not contain such a good Catholic-Protestant mix as the 10th. Volunteering would continue to be slow and there would never be enough Irishmen to keep existing units up to strength. With the exception of a Royal Dublin Fusiliers battalion, the 10th, which later went out to join the Royal Naval Division, no more active service wartime units would be raised in Ireland after the Ulster Division was formed. All existing Irish units would increasingly have to be made up with English reinforcements or face disbandment.

THE K3 DIVISIONS

The Army proceeded with the formation of the next group of six divisions. Even though the war was still not two months old, there were sufficient new battalions forming to complete these, but maintaining the Scottish, Irish, Northern, Eastern, Western and Light divisional titles was proving difficult. Some regions, particularly the heavily populated industrial areas, could have managed it; indeed there are

The Battle of Loos – hailed as a victory but indistinguishable from a defeat – blooded new divisions. A contemporary painting by a soldier who served here during the fighting.

signs in some of the next six divisions that a regional character was maintained. But the severe problems of recruiting in Ireland and sometimes in the less populated country areas on the mainland meant that there could be no overall regional basis in the organization of these next six divisions. They were all formed in September 1914.

21st Division

Formed around Tring in Hertfordshire entirely from battalions from North of England and Lincolnshire regiments. The division crossed to France on 7-15 September 1915 and was immediately thrown into action in the second phase of the Battle of Loos on the evening of 25 September. The story of how the division's traumatic experiences in this battle would be the cause of much change in the New Army will be described later. The division served on the Western Front until the Armistice, taking part in all of the major battles and suffering the highest number of casualties, over 55,000, in any New Army division.

22nd Division

Formed in camps around Eastbourne and Seaford on the Sussex coast from six Lancashire battalions, one each from Cheshire and Shropshire, and a complete brigade of Welsh battalions. Crossed to France in September 1915 and served briefly on the Western Front, but in October the division was transferred to Salonika where it remained until the Armistice. The division's war casualties, 7,728 men, were the

With the introduction of poisonous gas by the Germans at Ypres 1915, life in the trenches took a further nasty turn. Here a gun team take precautions against gas shells with primitive head protection.

British soldiers at their toiletries at a camp near Salonika. Life on the Salonika Front was less dangerous than on the Western Front or at Gallipoli.

lowest of any New Army division, illustrating the relative safety of the Salonika Front compared to France, Belgium and Gallipoli, and also illustrating how the chances of unit postings became life or death decisions for the men concerned.

23rd Division

Formed in the Aldershot area from battalions from Northumberland, Durham, Yorkshire and the Sherwood Foresters (the Notts and Derby Regiment in 1914). This would have been the 23rd (Northern) Division if the regional system had continued and it is probable that it had been originally organized with that in mind. I have seen references in print to that title.

The division crossed to France in August 1915. It went into action no less than five times in the Battle of the Somme in 1916. It also fought at Messines and in Third Ypres in 1917 but in November 1917 was transferred to the Italian Front where it served until the Armistice.

24th Division

Formed around Shoreham in Sussex entirely from battalions from the Eastern Counties, having been intended to be the 24th (Eastern) Division. Crossed to France in August and early September 1915 and, like the 21st Division, was thrown into the Battle of Loos on the evening of 25 September as a completely inexperienced division. Again, this will be referred to later.

A trench mortar team of the Seaforths on the Western Front. One of the team uses a periscope to observe the German trenches.

The division served on the Western Front until the Armistice, taking part in most of the great battles.

25th Division

Formed in the Salisbury area from battalions which should have become a Western Division. Crossed to France in September 1915. It fought in the Battle of the Somme several times from July to October 1916. Served on the Western Front until, like the 14th and 16th Divisions, it had to be returned to England briefly in the Summer of 1918 to be reconstituted. None of its original 'Western' battalions was present when the division returned to take part in the final campaigns.

26th Division

Formed in the Salisbury area with a variety of battalions, including a complete brigade of Scots and two Light Infantry battalions, the 8th Duke of Cornwall's and the 7th Oxfordshire and Buckinghamshire. Crossed to France in September 1915 but transferred to Salonika in November where it served for the remainder of the war, making four British divisions on that front – the 22nd, 26th, 27th and 28th Division, together with the 10th (Irish) Division from November 1915 until August 1917.

We now have thirty-one of our sixty-five active service divisions.

British troops in Salonika.

CHAPTER THREE

The Pals Divisions

The Army had already prepared the framework of its next group of six divisions – K4s – and allocated battalions forming at depots to them. But something was happening which caused a drastic change of plan. Before even the first month of war was over, local authorities and private bodies in many parts of the country had decided to help in building up the New Army.

The very first instance of this type of unit being formed took place in London when, on a day in August, possibly the 18th or 19th, some City businessmen asked Lieutenant-General Sir Henry Rawlinson to intercede with Kitchener about the possibility of their office-worker employees being able to enlist in the local regiment – the Royal Fusiliers – and serving in a new battalion reserved exclusively for them. Kitchener agreed and it was in this way that the 10th (Stockbrokers) Battalion, Royal Fusiliers, was formed. A prominent and vigorous nobleman, Lord Derby, became acquainted with this event and he asked Kitchener if local authorities could raise similar battalions, thus relieving the Army of the burden of housing, clothing and feeding

London stockbrokers on the morning that the Stock Exchange stopped trading on the outbreak of war. Sir Henry Rawlinson sought permission on the behalf of some of them to form a battalion exclusively for the office-worker employees. The 'Pals' phenomenon was born.

thousands of potential recruits. Kitchener agreed and a bargain was struck. The local authorities could go ahead, but they must become responsible for everything except the provision of weapons and the Army would not take over the units or reimburse any expenditure until ready to do so, which would not be until well into 1915. Lord Derby moved swiftly and the first of the new types of units were raised within only a few days, first in Lord Derby's home territory of Liverpool, then within hours at Manchester, and eventually right across the Industrial North and then the whole country, except Ireland which had different social and political circumstances.

Committees were rapidly formed, usually chaired by a Lord Mayor or a local MP or aristocrat. Recruiting offices were opened at Town Halls or suitable civilian buildings and a second flood of men now enlisted. Because the units being formed did not yet form part of the Army, they were not yet parts of regiments. They became 'City Battalions' or 'Pals Battalions' and I hope readers will not object if I sometimes use 'Pals' or 'Pals-type' to cover the whole privately raised unit movement. While men who were joining at the army depots became members of battalions drawn from the entire cross-section of the community and from the whole recruiting area of a regiment, the privately raised units came from individual cities and towns and frequently from narrow classes of men.

The Pals-type movement is usually looked back upon as a romantic, patriotic event, but it was not always in the Army's best interest. What

Impatient recruits outside Manchester Town Hall, 1 September 1914. Lord Derby had picked up on the idea of friends serving together in the same battalion for the duration of the war.

Leeds Pals taking the oath in the Victoria Hall, Leeds, September 1914.

The Lord Mayor of Liverpool, J E Rayner, Lord Kitchener and Lord Derby at a review of the Liverpool Pals, 20 March 1915.

started as a well-meant request by Rawlinson to Kitchener, giving just a thousand young office workers in London the chance to serve together, eventually led to many thousands of men segregating themselves into units according to class or occupation. Started as distinctly middle class with the Stockbrokers and many of the early City Battalions, the movement then spread to the upper class when five 'Public Schools Battalions' were formed, reserved for former public schoolboys. Those 5,000 former public schoolboys – nearly all potential officers and NCOs – deprived the Army of leadership material badly needed by the Army-raised battalions which were taking undue proportions of the labouring classes with whom the upper- and middle-class men clearly did not wish to mix. Some elements of the Pals movement owed as much to class prejudice as to patriotism.

The movement became widespread both in scale and in variety. There would eventually be everything in strength between a platoon of men who joined from a factory, workshop or office to a complete division when the Ulster Volunteer Force decided to become part of the British Army. A list to be included later shows the wide variety of organizations taking part in what often had all the characteristics of a crusade.

The Army's divisional numbering had reached the 26th Division with the completion of the K3 divisions. The next three numbers were allocated to the last Regular divisions created out of battalions brought back from overseas stations, so the Army had been ready to resume with

Volunteers from the 13th York and Lancasters (Barnsley Pals), about to join a Royal Engineer Tunnelling Company for duty at Hill 60, Belgium.

a 30th Division in its building up of the New Army. As has been stated, battalions forming at regimental depots had been allocated to the next group of six divisions, the K4s. But the flood of men for the Pals-type battalions in late 1914 and early 1915 reduced the numbers of men joining at depots. The War Office now decided to allocate locally raised units to virtually the whole of the twelve K4 and K5 divisions – which is why I like to call them 'Pals Divisions'. The original K4 divisional organizations were broken up in March 1915 and the seventy-two battalions originally allocated to those divisions mostly became reserve battalions which would remain in England to train and provide reinforcements for the first eighteen New Army divisions. When the Pals battalions were eventually taken over by the Army, they usually left behind a reserve company of surplus men which also became reserve battalions providing reinforcements for the twelve Pals divisions. These were all prudent moves which would maintain the strength of all of the New Army divisions when they went overseas.

It took up to a year before the Army was able to take over the Pals battalions, although they were given battalion numbers in regiments and allocated to brigades and divisions before then. The final twelve divisions would require 156 battalions (thirteen each now that a pioneer battalion became a standard feature) and eight more would be required as Pioneers for Regular divisions. Of those 164 battalions, the Army would provide only sixteen battalions and the Territorial Force would provide four.

Leeds Pals arrive at Colsterdale and are addressed by their commanding officer, Colonel Stead, September 1914.

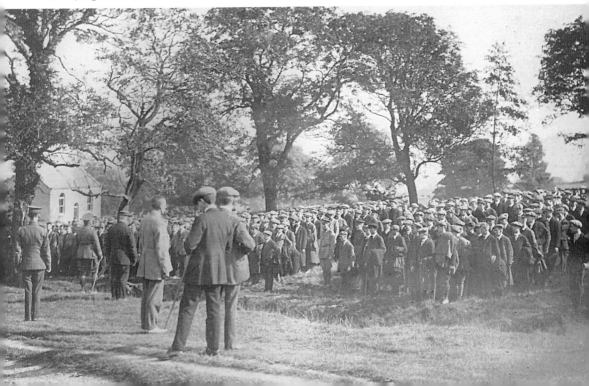

The 144 privately raised units can be broken down as follows:

City/Pals-type	96
Ulster Volunteer Force	13
Tyneside Scottish and Irish	8
Public Schools	5
Sportsmen	5
Commercials	3
Public Works Pioneers	3
Empire and Empire League	2
Boys Brigade, Church Lads Brigade	2
Others	7

The Sportsmen included the 1st and 2nd Football Battalions (the 17th and 23rd Middlesex). The Public Works Pioneers were also raised in Middlesex (the 18th, 19th and 26th Battalions). 'Commercials' were usually organized by Chambers of Commerce. The seven others were: North Eastern Railway Pioneers (17th Northumberland Fusiliers), West Yorkshire Wool Textile Pioneers (21st West Yorkshires), Glasgow Tramways (15th Highland Light Infantry), Stockbrokers (10th Royal Fusiliers), Bankers (26th Royal Fusiliers), Arts and Crafts (18th King's Royal Rifle Corps) and North Country Yeoman Rifles (21st King's Royal Rifle Corps).

The morale and spirit of comradeship of these battalions was of the highest order. It is tragic that the ability of those who would lead them in battle was not. The provision of commanders at divisional and

Footballers' Battalion at Church Parade at the White City Stadium, London, the service conducted by the Bishop of Birmingham, Dr Russell Wakefield.

brigade level, together with their staffs, and the key officers and NCOs in battalions was an inexorable drawing from deeper down into a supply that was steadily deteriorating. The proportion of dug-out officers increased; the over-rapid promotion of other officers took place. In the Pals battalions it was often the sons of local business or professional men who found themselves as immediately appointed junior officers, sometimes even as company commanders. John Harris's *Covenant with Death* provides a superb description of the formation of a typical battalion, in this case based on the Sheffield City Battalion, later to become the 12th York and Lancaster. One-eyed veteran Lieutenant-Colonel Pine, Captain Ashton, who became a company commander simply because of maturity of age, and boozy old-soldier Sergeant Corker, the commissionaire at the local newspaper office where many of the characters in the book worked before joining up and where Captain Ashton was chief reporter, are all representative of the men who had to make soldiers out of the Pals.

Left: *Colonel Hughes commanding the Sheffield City Battalion – a 'dugout'.* **Below:** *Recruits for the Sheffield City Battalion drilling with a few precious obsolete rifles.*

SHEFFIELD UNIVERSITY
AND
CITY SPECIAL BATTALION

Col. Hughes, C.B., C.M.G., Acting Commandant.

Capt. E. A. Marples, Acting Adjutant.

For Professional Men,
For Business Men,
For Teachers,
For Clerks,
For Shop Assistants,
Etc., Etc.

Enrolment at the Town Hall
TO-DAY,
10 a.m. to 7 p.m.

ENROL NOW.

THE K4 DIVISIONS

30th Division

Formed as the 37th Division in late 1914 but renumbered 30th in April 1915. An all-Lancashire division made up of eight Manchester and four Liverpool Pals battalions. One Manchester battalion later became a Bantam (a unit made up of men below the normal minimum height for recruits but otherwise of good physique) and was transferred to the 35th Division in 1915, being replaced by the Oldham Pals (24th Manchesters). The St Helens Pals (11th South Lancashire) joined in 1915 as a pioneer battalion. The artillery and Royal Engineers were also from Lancashire. Lord Derby had taken the initiative in forming many of the division's units and it is possible that it was his influence that persuaded the War Office to make this the senior of the Pals divisions, a reasonable decision because the Manchester and Liverpool battalions had been among the first of the Pals to form.

The division assembled at Grantham in April 1915 but was not complete in supporting units until September. Crossed to France in October. A brigade of Manchesters was then exchanged with a Regular brigade of the 7th Division; the reason for this type of exchange will be described later. The division's first battle was the opening day of the 1916 Battle of the Somme when it took all of its objectives, including Montauban, the first village to be captured in the battle. Served on the Western Front until nearly wiped out in the German offensives on the Somme and the Lys in March and April 1918. The division was out of

Men of 25th Battalion (Reserve), The Manchester Regiment, marching past Lord Kitchener in front of Manchester Town Hall.

action for two months while being reorganized and, when it returned to take part in the successful attacks in the closing months of the war, five of the nine battalions were London Territorials and only one Lancashire battalion, the 2nd South Lancashire, was present.

31st Division

Formed as the 38th Division, became 31st in April 1915. Made up of eleven Pals-type battalions from Yorkshire and one each from Lancashire and Durham. A complete brigade was made up of four battalions from Hull, having been raised by the East Riding Territorial Force Association. The Association had easily completed its Territorial recruitment requirements and went on to provide these four battalions for the New Army. The Hull battalions were known locally as the Commercials, the Tradesmen, the Sportsmen and 'T'Others'. The other Yorkshire battalions were two each from Bradford and Barnsley and one each from Leeds, Sheffield and Halifax. The single Lancashire battalion was the Accrington Pals (11th East Lancashire). The Durham Pals (18th Durham Light Infantry) were at West Hartlepool on 15 December 1914 and suffered six fatal casualties when four German warships shelled the town. The Durhams' dead were the first casualties in a New Army division.

The men of many units had to remain at home and train locally until camps were provided and the division did not assemble, at Ripon, until June 1915. The division sailed for Egypt in December 1915 and briefly

Men of the 15th West Yorkshires, The Leeds Pals, on a route march in North Yorkshire in 1915.

manned defence positions on the Suez Canal, but was soon transferred to France, arriving at Marseilles in March 1916. First battle: on the extreme left wing of the Fourth Army main attack front on the opening day of the Battle of the Somme. The attack failed with heavy casualties. The division served on the Western Front until the Armistice.

32nd Division

Formed as the 39th Division, became 32nd in April 1915. The infantry were all Pals-type units: three battalions each from Glasgow, Birmingham and Salford, two from Newcastle and one each from Bristol and Westmorland-Cumberland. The Glasgow battalions were known as the Tramways, the Boys Brigade and the Commercial Battalions, the Newcastle ones as the Commercials and the Railway Pals. The Westmorland-Cumberland battalion (11th Border) was known as the Lonsdales after its raiser, Lord Lonsdale.

After moving from camp to camp in England for more than a year, the division crossed to France in November 1915 and almost immediately lost the Birmingham and Bristol battalions in an exchange of Regulars with the 5th Division. First battle: the opening day of the Battle of the Somme attacking Thiepval without success. The division served on the Western Front until the Armistice.

Men of the 16th Lancashire Fusiliers, 2nd Salford Pals.

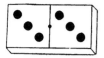

33rd Division

Formed as the 40th Division, becoming 33rd in April 1915. This was an all-London division with five Public Schools battalions, (18th to 21st Royal Fusiliers and 16th Middlesex); two Sportmens, an 'Empire' and a Kensington battalion (all Royal Fusiliers); West Ham (13th Essex), 1st Football (17th Middlesex) and Church Lads Brigade (16th King's Royal Rifle Corps); the pioneer battalion was known as the 1st Public Works (18th Middlesex). The divisional artillery was raised at Camberwell and the Royal Engineer units at Tottenham.

The division assembled at Clipstone Camp in Nottinghamshire in July 1915 and crossed to France in November 1915. The division was considerably reorganized after its arrival in France. No less than six battalions were exchanged with Regulars of the 2nd Division; another went to the 29th Division and three of the Royal Fusiliers Public Schools battalions were disbanded, with most of their members being persuaded to accept commissions. The Army thus gained around 3,000 new officers who otherwise would have been happy to continue as privates in Kitchener's Army. The only original battalions remaining were the 3rd Public Schools, the Church Lads Brigade and the Public Works battalion; the infantry of the division now became more Regular then New Army.

The division took part in the Battle of the Somme in mid-July 1916 at High Wood, where it has at least two small battalion memorials, and continued to serve on the Western Front until the Armistice.

Men of the 24th Royal Fusiliers, the 2nd Sportsman's Battalion, during training at Hare Hall Camp, Romford, Essex.

34th Division

Formed as the 41st Division, became 34th in April 1915. The infantry were all Pals-type: four battalions each Tyneside Irish and Tyneside Scottish, two Edinburgh City, the Cambridge Battalion (11th Suffolks) and the Grimsby Chums (10th Lincolns); the pioneer battalion was known as the 1st Tyneside Pioneers (18th Northumberland Fusiliers). The artillery came from Nottingham, Sunderland, Staffordshire and Leicestershire, and the Royal Engineers from Norfolk.

The division was not able to assemble until August 1915, on Salisbury Plain, and it crossed to France in January 1916. It escaped the exchange of battalions with Regular divisions and fought its first battle with all of its original units on the opening day of the Battle of the Somme, attacking in the centre of the Fourth Army front against La Boisselle. Only small gains were made and at terrible cost; the division's casualties – 6,380 men – were the highest of the day, being over 1,000 more than the next highest (29th Division – 5,240 men). Included in the casualties were seven of the eight Tyneside Scottish and Irish battalion commanders and the brigade commander of the Tyneside Irish.

The division served continually on the Western Front until 1918 when, like the 30th Division, it almost ceased to exist after the German offensives on the Somme and the Lys and had to be reconstituted. All the original battalions disappeared and the division's infantry was

Men of the Tyneside Irish caught by the camera on their way to attack the German trenches at La Boisselle, 7.30 am Saturday morning 1 July, 1916.

almost entirely Territorial in the final months. The division's war casualties numbered 37,404, the highest total in the Pals divisions.

35th (Bantam) Division

Formed as the 42nd Division, became 35th in April 1915. The infantry (but not other divisional units) were allowed to recruit otherwise fit men below the normal Army minimum height of five feet, three inches, down to a new minimum for these 'Bantams' of five feet, though men even below this height sometimes managed to be accepted. The recruiting was all carried out by private raisers, so these units were all of the Pals type. They came from: South-East Lancashire, Salford, Manchester, Birkenhead, West of England (14th Gloucesters), Nottingham, Edinburgh, Leeds, West Hartlepool and Glasgow; the pioneer battalion was the 2nd Tyneside Pioneers.

The division assembled in North Yorkshire in June-July 1915 and crossed to France in early 1916. The infantry had one advantage when holding trenches; its men suffered fewer head wounds, but they needed an extra sandbag on the firestep when required to man the parapet. The division fought well on the Somme in the Delville Wood area in July and August 1916 but could not obtain sufficient reinforcements of both good physique and Bantam height. Inspections in December 1916 found 2,784 men to be of unacceptable physique and they were posted out of the division. The battalions then ceased to be purely Bantams and took in reinforcements of normal height, many of the first intake

Men of the 16th Cheshires, 2nd Birkenhead Bantams. The minimum height was five feet, although smaller men managed to get accepted.

being men who had volunteered for the Yeomanry (Territorial cavalry). But the division retained its original units and served on the Western Front until the Armistice.

THE K5 DIVISIONS

The final six of the thirty-division New Amy planned by Kitchener were formed without too much difficulty. There would always be problems about finding suitable commanders and staff, and these last divisions had to draw from the bottom of the well. But voluntary enlistments for the new units held up well; Kitchener had not misjudged the spirit of the country. This last phase was boosted by the presentation intact of virtually two complete divisions of infantry from Ulster and Wales. Most of these last units would continue to be formed by private initiative, leaving the divisions to be taken over by the Army at a later date. These are the last six New Army divisions.

36th (Ulster) Division

The infantry in this division was provided almost exclusively by the Ulster Volunteer Force, a pre-war force of what would now be called paramilitaries prepared to fight anyone – the British Army or Irish Nationalists – who tried to force them into an all-Ireland Home Rule governed from Dublin and with a Catholic majority. The UVF (which still exists as I write in 1999) contained 80,000 men between the ages of seventeen and sixty-five, was armed and formed into local units. On

Right: *Blessing the Colours of the 10th Royal Irish Rifles, the South Belfast Volunteers.*

Below: *Men of the 15th Royal Irish Rifles, the North Belfast Volunteers, being inspected by Sir Edward Carson.*

Opposite above: *The Royal Irish after a succesful fight on the Western Front in 1917 wave items captured from the enemy.*

Opposite below: *The Duke of Connaught inspects Irish troops on the Western Front in the summer of 1916, during the Battle of the Somme.*

the outbreak of war an unwritten political truce over Home Rule was established, with Ulster being told that no changes would be made while the war was being fought. Kitchener immediately asked the Ulster politicians if they would bring the younger men of the UVF into his New Army. The Ulster leaders agreed, after only a short delay, but insisted that their men should serve together in one division and that the word 'Ulster' should be contained in the divisions's title. This was eventually accepted, much to the disappointment of the Home Rule enthusiasts who wanted to see an all-Ireland force of three divisions based on Dublin, Belfast and Cork. So the two 'Irish' divisions – the 10th and 16th – were formed, as we have seen, but they never became all-Ireland in character and the Ulstermen obtained their own separate division.

The younger men in the UVF came forward immediately and its area units formed the basis of battalions of those Irish regiments which traditionally recruited in Ulster. The War Office could not see, initially, where the division would fit into the organization of the New Army, so it remained simply the Ulster Division until late October 1914 when it became the 36th (Ulster) Division. Most of the division's supporting units were also formed in Ulster, but the British Government would not allow Ulster artillery units to form; the risk that the guns might be used by the UVF after the war could not be taken. The division's artillery was provided by mainland Britain.

The division came to England in July 1915, concentrating at Seaford

in Sussex, and in October crossed to France. Its first battle was on the opening day of the Battle of the Somme when the division succeeded in making a good but isolated advance near Thiepval and was forced back by German counter-attacks. It was acknowledged that the division had performed well; four Victoria Crosses were awarded. The division's memorial – the Ulster Tower – stands on the German front line captured that day. But casualties had been heavy and this episode probably counted in Ulster's favour when its Protestant population benefitted from the partition of Ireland after the war. The division served on the Western Front until the Armistice, taking part in every one of the big battles of 1917 and 1918. But its Ulster content steadily diminished because conscription was not introduced into Ireland and men from the mainland had to be drafted in to maintain its strength. It is a matter of record that there was never any trouble between Protestants in the 36th Division and Catholics in the 16th Division at any time when they served together on the Western Front; indeed the two divisions took part in the capture of the Messines Ridge in June 1917, advancing side-by-side in a successful attack. A new 'all-Ireland' war memorial tower was erected at Messines in 1998.

37th Division

The origins of this division do not fit in with the Pals-type nature of the other K4 and K5 divisions. When the first three groups of New Army divisions were being formed from men brought directly into the

Catholic (16th) and Protestant (36th) Divisions fought side by side at Messines Ridge in June 1917. After the successful attack the Irish consolidate their gains.

Army by the first wave of volunteering, the War Office kept some of the early New Army battalions out of the first eighteen divisions formed; they became 'Army Troops', spares to be used later for unforeseen eventualities. One such occurred when it was thought that the proposed 16th (Irish) Division might not succeed in forming. Twelve of these Army Troops battalions were gathered together and given the provisional title of 44th Division, ready to replace the 16th Division in the K2 group of divisions. But the 16th did form; the 44th was kept intact and became the 37th Division in this K5 group. Among its diverse cross-section of infantry battalions there was a complete Leicesters brigade (the 6th to 9th Battalions); Leicestershire had been one of the 'orphan' counties left out of the regional divisional organization of the early New Army. Another battalion was the 10th Royal Fusiliers, or Stockbrokers Battalion, which had been the very first example of a Pals battalion when businessmen in the City of London had persuaded Kitchener, through Rawlinson, to allow office workers to enlist together in August 1914.

With such early origins the division was comparatively well officered and equipped when it concentrated on the Salisbury Plain in April 1915. It crossed to France in July 1915.

The division had an unusual introduction to the Western Front battles. It was not called upon to take part in a major attack until the end of the first week of the 1916 Battle of the Somme, when battalions of the division were sent into action under the command of another

A battalion of the Leicesters on parade prior to departure for France in July 1915. It was to be a year later before they took part in a major attack during the Battle of the Somme.

division and the same thing happened in November in the closing stages of the Somme. In the interval, the Leicester brigade was exchanged with a brigade of the 21st Division, another New Army formation. All of these events suggested that there was some difficulty over the leadership of the division. The first divisional commander was Major-General Count Gleichen who was allowed by the King to drop the Germanic 'Count' and be known as Lord Gleichen. (He was the son of a princely German admiral and of the daughter of an English admiral and held British citizenship. He was not a 'dug-out' general but a fifty-three-years-old Regular officer with a Guards background and had seen much hard fighting as a brigade commander with the BEF in 1914.) Major-General Gleichen never did command his division in battle; he was succeeded by another commander in October, but that officer was invalided home within three weeks and, when the division went into action again, in November on the Ancre, it was once again split up with its brigades attached to other divisions. A new commander soon arrived and he took the division through to the Armistice, with the division fighting well in the 1917 and 1918 battles.

38th (Welsh) Division

The original Welsh intention, decided upon at a meeting on 28 September 1914, was to provide a Welsh Corps of two divisions for the New Army. It was realized later in the year, however, that this proposal was too ambitious, so the new units being raised by private initiative in

Royal Welsh Fusiliers at camp at Rhyl. Lloyd George was very active in the creation of the all-Welsh division.

Wales were formed into a single division designated 43rd (Welsh) in December but renumbered in April 1915. Virtually every unit in the original division was raised by local committees in Wales and it was a veritable all-Welsh division, although some later additions of artillery came from outside sources. Lloyd George was very active in its creation and the Army was persuaded to place many of his nominees in command positions. The division was sometimes called 'Lloyd George's Welsh Army'.

The division came from its early camps throughout Wales and finally assembled at Winchester in August 1915 before crossing to France in December. Its first major battle was a gruelling experience. On 7 July 1916 the division was given the task of attacking the large expanse of Mametz Wood to allow the next phase of the Somme offensive to proceed. Three battalions attacked but were beaten back with heavy loss. The local corps commander then demanded that the divisional commander – one of Lloyd George's placements – be removed, and it was under a fresh commander sent from another division that the wood was attacked again three days later. This time the division did clear the wood in hard fighting, defeating two crack German regiments and enabling a successful major attack to commence on this sector. The division suffered 4,000 casualties and its memorial, a red dragon, now stands on a bluff overlooking Mametz Wood.

The division was not called upon to mount an attack again until the opening day of Third Ypres, 31 July 1917, when it made a good advance

A Brigadier General confers with his officers in Mametz Wood after its capture. The 38th (Welsh) Division attacked successfully in July 1916. Men of the 38th in the winter of 1917.

on the Pilckem sector and captured all of its objectives. It was fortunate in not being involved in the German March Offensive in 1918 and emerged in good heart to take part in the successful battles of the Advance to Victory period leading to the Armistice.

39th Division

This division was formed in the Winchester area in August 1915 from thirteen Pals-type battalions, among them three Sussex battalions (known as the 1st to 3rd South Downs), four from London (raised by St Pancras, Wandsworth, Shoreditch and Islington), two from Nottinghamshire and Derbyshire (the Chatsworth Rifles and the Welbeck Rangers), battalions from Portsmouth (the 14th Hampshire) and the Forest of Dean (the 13th Gloucesters), a British Empire League battalion (the 17th King's Royal Rifles Corps) and another from the Argyll and Sutherland Highlanders.

The last-formed brigade in the division, comprising the Wandsworth, Shoreditch and Islington battalions and the Argyll and Sutherland Highlanders, was not judged sufficiently well trained when the division went to France in March 1916 and was replaced by four Territorial battalions transferred from other divisions already serving on the Western Front. The division went into battle in September 1916 on the Somme on the Ancre sector (see the account by Edmund Blunden in *Undertones of War*; he was in one of the Sussex battalions) and served on the Western Front until April 1918, taking part in Third Ypres in 1917

NCOs and officers of the 11th Royal Sussex, the 1st South Downs, in 1917. The poet Edmund Blunden served with this battalion.

and facing the German offensives on the Somme and on the Lys in
March and April 1918, but the division emerged so weak in strength
from these that it had to become non-operational and was reduced to a
framework for the remainder of the war, mainly involved in the training
of newly arrived American divisions.

40th Division

This division was formed in the Aldershot area in September 1915
and was intended to be a second Bantam division. But when the
battalions arrived it was found that too many men were not only under
height but were also undersized and were deemed unsuitable for active
service. Four Welsh Bantam battalions, containing many coalminers,
were almost totally acceptable, but the other eight battalions were
reduced by amalgamation to four, from Lancashire, Glasgow, Suffolk
and North Yorkshire. The resulting shortage of four battalions was made
up by the taking in of the four Pals battalions of the 39th Division
whose training had not been sufficiently far advanced for them to go to
France with that division. With the addition of a Teesside pioneer
battalion (the 12th Green Howards), the division was now ready for
service and crossed to France in June 1916.

It was present for the final phase of the Somme in November 1916,
but its first big battle was not until Cambrai in November 1917. After
facing the German attacks on the Somme and the Lys in 1918, the
division had to be reduced to a training cadre for a few weeks until

*Welsh Bantams employed in carrying up supplies to the front line. Mainly hardy ex-
coalminers, these small-sized soldiers were found physically acceptable for active service.*

made up to strength again with ten new battalions sent from England. This enabled the division to take part in the Advance to Victory campaign, but with not one of its original battalions present at that time.

41st Division

This division, the last of the New Army, was formed at Aldershot in September 1915 from Pals-type battalions – eleven from London and Southern England designated variously as Bermondsey, Lewisham, Battersea, East Ham, Lambeth, Portsmouth, Kent County, the 2nd Football Battalion (23rd Middlesex), the Arts and Crafts Battalion (18th King's Royal Rifle Corps), the Bankers (26th Royal Fusiliers), and the Middlesex Public Works Pioneers and two battalions from the North – the Yeoman Rifles (21st King's Royal Rifle Corps) and the Wearside Battalion (20th Durham Light Infantry).

The division crossed to France in May 1916 and was fortunate that its introduction to battle took place on 15 September on the Somme, the day when the first use of tanks took the Germans by surprise. The division took all of its objectives, including the village of Flers where its impressive memorial now stands in the main street up which a tank was reported to have driven followed by a crowd of cheering infantry from the division. This division, and the 18th and 30th Divisions on the opening day of the Somme, were the only ones of the thirty New Army divisions to achieve unqualified successes at reasonable cost in their first major actions.

The division served on the Western Front until the Armistice, taking part in every one of the major battles still to be fought, although it was absent for a short period in Italy from November 1917 to March 1918. It managed to maintain its original composition almost unchanged to the end.

This concludes the listing of the successful formation of the thirty divisions of the New Army and reaches number forty-three of our sixty-five active service infantry divisions.

43

65

Officers belonging to the 41st Division consult a map during their four month period in Italy in 1917 - 1918.

Chapter Four

The New Army Goes to War

The New Army divisions were not rushed into action without reasonable preparation. Unlike volunteer German divisions, which were fighting within a month of their formation in 1914, the average New Army division had about a ten-month training period before being sent to a theatre of active operations. On at least one crisis occasion, in November 1914, Kitchener refused French cries for help and would not allow any of his new divisions to leave England prematurely. When they did go, they went with the doubts of some but the high hopes of many that this fine force of patriotic volunteers, in physique the equal of the pre-war Regulars and in average intellect superior to them, would do well. Given good commanders they might have done, but the introduction into battle of the first batch of the new divisions often proved to be a traumatic and unsatisfactory experience and would lead to some drastic changes. Three names of three battles would be of particular importance for the reputation of the New Army – Gallipoli, Loos and the Somme.

Soldiers, lined up by company, await their turn to board a cross-Channel troopship likely bound for the French port of Boulogne.

Gallipoli

Three of the first six New Army divisions – the K1s – were sent to take part in the Gallipoli campaign. The 13th (Western) Division was in action first, fighting on the Anzac sector, but the 10th (Irish) and 11th (Northern) were allocated to what should have been a master stroke. After the front had stagnated on the Helles and Anzac sectors, a major third landing was planned at a comparatively undefended third place, Suvla Bay, on 6 August. The full-strength, fresh, Irish and Northern Divisions carried out this operation which, though performed in some confusion, took place with hardly a shot being fired by the Turkish defence.

But there then took place a delay of many hours before the troops were pushed forward to take advantage of the surprise. The Turks rushed in their reserves and the last chance to bring success from the Gallipoli campaign was lost. It was a terrible start for the New Army in its first major action. The blame was, justifiably, put on the commanders concerned and, in a famous cable, General Sir Ian Hamilton, the Gallipoli Commander-in-Chief, informed the War Office that he wanted replacements for the corps commander concerned and for both divisional commanders. The new commanders, all with experience of the Western Front, were duly sent out, but it was too late to salvage anything from the setback and too late for the New Army to remove an initial impression given as being a force that might not be reliable.

British infantry attacking the Turkish lines at Gallipoli. When the Irish and Northern Divisions had some success in their landing at Suvla Bay it was not followed up.

Loos

Just seven weeks later, on 25 September 1915, four other New Army divisions would face a fiercer test at Loos, a test much closer to home and subject to scrutiny. The 9th (Scottish) and 15th (Scottish) Divisions were chosen (by a fellow Scot, Haig, the army commander directing this battle) to be two of the four divisions carrying out the main part of the opening attack at Loos. Two more divisions, the 21st and 24th – K3s, were allocated to the reserve force which was to push through the anticipated gap in the German lines created in the first phase and become a pursuit force marching deep into the German rear. This 'pursuit force' was a highly optimistic concept and the allocation to it of the 21st and 24th Divisions highly questionable, because both divisions had only recently arrived in France and had never even taken a turn at trench-holding duty. They were selected on the assumption that completely fresh troops, not burdened with the lethargy of trench holding, would be vigorous in the hoped-for pursuit. (If regional subtitles had been allocated to the K3 divisions, the 21st would have been 'Northern' and the 24th 'Eastern'.)

The two Scottish divisions did well in the opening attack. The 9th captured the German front-line trench and pushed on to reach the second line, but could not penetrate it. The 15th captured the village of Loos and rushed on to seize a vital height, Hill 70, making the deepest advance of the day, but became involved in hand-to-hand fighting with Germans coming out from their second-line trench and pushing the

A depiction of the attack at Loos by war artist Matania. The two Scottish divisions did well at the outset of the assault.

Scots off Hill 70 and back to the edge of Loos village. Twelve divisions eventually took part in the Battle of Loos but the casualties of the two Scottish divisions on that first day were the two highest in the whole battle and it was this cost that was to be the cause of changes being made later to these two divisions.

The circumstances of the handling of the raw 21st and 24th Divisions were quite different and were to be further reaching in their effects. They had been held too far back (the decision of the Commander-in Chief, Sir John French), were pushed up in chaotic manner (poor staff work), and arrived tired and sometimes hungry in pouring rain and in the dark, to be told that they were to go forward to exploit a gap which, in fact, did not exist. Both divisions were caught unprepared when German forces infiltrated between the leading battalions early the following morning, leaving the British units confused, split up and under heavy attack. In this highly unfavourable situation, parts of units started to fall back and eventually most of both divisions withdrew in what was little more than a rout, losing much of the ground captured by other divisions in the previous day's fighting. Casualties were of medium scale, nearly 4,000 for each division, but more importantly the action of these two divisions was judged to have disgraced the New Army.

Let us first deal with the effects of the battle on the two Scottish divisions. They had suffered over 12,000 casualties, 5,868 in the 9th Division and 6,668 in the 15th Division. This was at a time when

British wounded after an attack near Loos return to a dressing station. Disappointing performance by the 21st and 24th Divisions raised doubts about the New Army.

volunteering in Scotland was slackening, due to no more than a population insufficient to support the many Scottish units created, and there were insufficient trained reinforcements for such a sudden loss. No blame was laid on the commanders. (The commander of the 15th Division held his position for a further two years, but Major-General G.H. Thesiger of the 9th Division, appointed only two weeks before the battle, was killed on the third day of it.)

The infantry content of the two divisions had to be reorganized, a process facilitated by the fact that each division had sister battalions in the other. Men from the 9th Division were transferred to the 15th to bring the 15th up to strength again. No battalion lost its identity completely, four merged battalions being formed – 6th/7th Royal Scots Fusiliers, 7th/8th King's Own Scottish Borderers, 10th/11th Highland Light Infantry and 8th/10th Gordon Highlanders. That left the 9th Division short of a complete brigade. These changes took place in May 1916. Fortunately a brigade of fresh troops had just come to France. This was the South African Brigade, all volunteers, who arrived at the Western Front and were welcomed by the 9th Division as its third brigade. A few weeks later the division fought its next battle at Delville Wood on the Somme, where a South African memorial now stands – all because of the heavy Scots casualties at Loos. (The South Africans served in the 9th Division until September 1918 when they were transferred to another division at a time when the pressure of the final months of the war was causing many changes.)

A street in the coal mining village of Loos with the twin pit headgear in the background. The steel structure was referred to as 'Tower Bridge' and 'Crystal Palace' by the soldiers.

The effects of the experiences of the 21st and 24th Divisions were more drastic. The hard fighting and the success of the K1 9th and K2 15th Divisions on the first day at Loos gave evidence that at least some of these early New Army units were sufficiently trained and officered, but the retirement of the K3 21st and 24th Divisions on the second morning seemed to indicate that these later divisions were ill prepared, badly led and unreliable. Insufficient weight was given at the time to the fact that the C.-in-C. had kept them too far back and that bad staff work had brought these divisions onto the scene of battle tired and badly prepared. The realisation that the divisions had been held too far back came later and it was the ostensible reason for Sir John French losing his position as C.-in-C. at the end of the year, opening the way for Haig.

It was clear, however, that the quality of officers in these two K3 divisions was, through no more than a shortage of suitable material, not sufficiently high for active service on the Western Front. They were no more than the inevitable victims of the rapid expansion of divisions. The Official Historian* carried out research into the officer composition of the two divisions.

He found that only one of the two divisional commanders, only two of the eight brigade commanders (six infantry and two artillery) and only one of twenty-six battalion commanders were Regulars; all the rest

* *Military Operations, France and Belgium, 1915 Volume II*, pages 293-4.

Walking wounded from the battle of Loos about to board a train to take them to a Base Hospital. The Commander-in-Chief Sir John French was held responsible for keeping reserve divisions too far back resulting in their being brought into the attack ill prepared. He lost his position as C-in-C three months later; he was 63 years old.

But if the K3 divisions were suspect, what of the K4s and 5s – the Pals divisions? The first three of these to have arrived in France – the 30th, 32nd and 33rd – also carried out brigade exchanges with Regular divisions, the 31st Division escaping this process only because it was temporarily in Egypt. Only the 1st and 4th Divisions of the Regulars in the BEF at that time were not affected by these changes and remained completely Regular in composition, possibly because they had been earmarked to exchange brigades with the two New Army divisions sent to Salonika. But this would leave the last eight New Army divisions – 34th to 41st – and the 31st when it came back from Egypt, all to take part in their first battles without the benefit of such Regular infusion.

The Somme

The effects on the New Army of this next battle, which would rage for 140 days from July to November 1916 compared with the Loos battle of less than three weeks, can be described more briefly, although its impact would be many times greater and more enduring than the New Army's baptisms of battle at Gallipoli and Loos.

Unlike the earlier groups of New Army divisions which had been dispersed to various fighting fronts, every single one of the K4 and K5 Pals-type divisions went to the Western Front and all fought their first battles on the Somme and suffered severe casualties there. Five of them, the 31st at Serre, the 36th (Ulster) and 32nd at Thiepval, the 34th at La Boisselle and the 30th at Montauban, took part in the disastrous first

Men of the 10th East Yorks, The Hull Commercials, 31st Division, at the opening stages of the Battle of the Somme.

day on 1 July. Because of the Pals aspect of most of the infantry units in these divisions, the heavy casualties suffered in one or two days of fighting made a huge impact, not upon a county or a region as in the earlier battalions raised at Army depots, but in individual cities and towns. Furthermore, there had been a bond of comradeship in the Pals battalions stronger than in the earlier New Army ones. Heavy casualties therefore made a greater emotional impact both upon the surviving soldiers and in the communities at home which lost so many men at one time. It is for this reason that the Somme, and particularly the first day when 21,392 men were killed and 35,493 were wounded, haunts the memory of the First World War in Great Britain and Ireland. It is for this reason that hundreds gather at the Lochnagar Crater at La Boisselle and sometimes thousands at the Thiepval Memorial to the Missing on 1st of July anniversaries.*

It is ironic that the army officer who negotiated between the City of London businessmen and Kitchener to allow the office workers to serve together in the 10th Royal Fusiliers, which set in train the Pals movement in 1914, was General Sir Henry Rawlinson under the command of whose Fourth Army most of the Pals went into battle on the Somme.

* See the author's *The First Day on the Somme*, Penguin, for a description of the first day's fighting.

The Pals system of forming battalions from men living in the same area ensured that maximum distress occurred for communities in this country, following a major battle.

MANY YORKSHIREMEN KILLED.

£3,50

HEAVY LOSSES AMONGST LEEDS BATTALIONS.

THE PALS' LONG DEATH-ROLL.

WELL-KNOWN HEADINGLEY DOCTOR'S SON DANGEROUSLY WOUNDED.

To-day's list of casualties, which is particularly distressing to Leeds by reason of the long catalogue of killed among the Leeds Pals, relates almost exclusively to casualties sustained in the Allies' great offensive on the Western front since July 1.

Another Leeds officer reported killed is Sec.-Lieut. Herbert Parsons, of the 2nd Royal Scots, who enlisted as a private at the beginning of the war. After attaining sergeant's rank, he obtained a commission and went out to France in September, 1915. He was wounded on December 5, and on returning to France, was killed on July 16. He was formerly a pupil of the Leeds Modern School, and gained an honours B.A. at London University, and was a well-known player of the Wakefield Rugby football club. His parents, Mr. and

Garforth. He was employed at the City Treasurer's Office, was an old Parish Church choir boy, and was educated at the Middle Class School. He was keenly interested in sport, being a member of the Garforth Golf Club. In a letter to his parents, a comrade says of Pte. Burnley:—"There was not a better soldier in the battalion, as, efficient himself, he did his best to get others to take a pride in their work. . . . He was second to none, not only in physique but as a soldier and bomber. . . . A true friend, he was always willing to do a good turn and help anyone who was down."

Mrs. Cawood, 9, Wilmington Grove, Leeds, has been informed by letter from the chaplain of the death of her husband, Private F. Cawood, machine-gun section. Previous to joining he was employed for many years by Messrs. J. Hepworth and Sons (Ltd.), clothiers, Clay Pit Lane, Leeds, as book-keeper. He leaves one son, aged 4 years, and was 34 years of age.

Information has now been received that Signaller R. W. Priestley, previously reported missing, was killed in action on July 1st. He joined the Pals Battalion on its formation, and previous to enlistment he was engaged at Messrs. Hyam and Co. (Ltd.), Briggate, Leeds. He was 22 years of age, and his relatives live at 7, Broomfield Road, Headingley.

Private ___ rence Iles, who was only 16½ years old, was killed in action on July 1st. He belonged to B Company, and was the son of Mrs. Iles, 7, Spenceley Street, Woodhouse Lane. His father, the late Mr. William Iles, served through the Afghanistan campaign.

Official news has been received of the death of Pte. T. Herbert Heaton, Leeds Pals, on July 1st. He had

JUDGE

In the asked to a Holbrook. Bil and battleship December five lines

The Me men, but on board a man rating the Victo exploit.

Mr. D. of the cla battleship Holbrook to get thr Dardanell

Lieut. the senior attempt.

Witness minutes, the water. marine o managed

New Army Divisional Casualties

When the Official Historians prepared their volumes, *Order of Battle of Divisions,* the team responsible for the thirty New Army divisions included the number of casualties – killed, wounded and missing – for each of those divisions. Unfortunately the same work was not carried out on the Regular and Territorial divisions. By using the New Army casualties, however, it is possible to produce the following table which illustrates which divisions experienced the hardest fighting. Account should be taken of the progressively later date of arrival at the front of the higher numbered divisions.

Divisions	Casualties	Fronts	Approximate Casualties per Month on Active Service
21st	55,581	Western Front	1,490
9th (Scottish)	52,055	Western Front	1,260
25th	48,289	Western Front	1,408
18th (Eastern)	46,503	Western Front	1,183
15th (Scottish)	45,542	Western Front	1,159
12th (Eastern)	41,363	Western Front	1,026
34th	41,183	Western Front	1,316
17th (Northern)	40,258	Western Front	1,024
19th (Western)	39,381	Western Front	1,002
33rd	37,404	Western Front	1,090
14th (Light)	37,100	Western Front	969
20th (Light)	35,470	Western Front	903
24th	35,362	Western Front	948
30th	35,182	Western Front	1,066
32nd	34,226	Western Front	970
36th (Ulster)	32,186	Western Front	887
11th (Northern)	32,165	Gallipoli/Western Front	1,011
41st	32,158	Western Front/Italy	1,098
31st	30,091	Western Front	961
37th	29,969	Western Front	763
38th (Welsh)	28,635	Western Front	835
16th (Irish)	28,398	Western Front	835
39th	27,869	Western Front	890
35th (Bantam)	23,915	Western Front	727
23rd	23,574	Western Front	616
40th	19,179	Western Front	678
13th (Western)	12,656	Gallipoli/Mesopotamia	350
10th (Irish)	9,363	Gallipoli/Salonika/Palestine	258
26th	8,022	Western Front/Salonika	215
22nd	7,728	Western Front/Salonika	215

The German Volunteer Experience

Because of the German conscription system, with all able-bodied men aged twenty to twenty-two serving their period of compulsory service and men above that age liable to recall as Reservists, there was only limited scope in Germany for a Kitchener-type wartime expansion using volunteers. But the Germans did call for volunteers on the outbreak of war, the appeal going out to young men aged seventeen to nineteen, asking them to join up rather than wait to reach the normal age of conscription. The result, mainly among students of the better educated classes, is strikingly depicted in Remarque's book, *All Quiet on the Western Front*.

Under much pressure, particularly from their school and college teachers, approximately 200,000 youths enlisted and were absorbed into new local units. They received fourteen days' recruit training, ten days' platoon training and a short period of company and battalion training. Their officers and NCOs were Reservists, often their old teachers, and each company was given at least seventy-five older Reservists. Thirteen new divisions were created from units which included a high proportion of these young volunteers. After little more than two months, they were sent into action in October 1914 in Germany's desperate bid to avoid being drawn into a prolonged war. Two divisions went to the Russian Front, one to Lorraine and ten to Flanders, where four of them came up against the skilled musketry of the BEF in front of Ypres.

German youths in training: The **Kriegsfreiwilliger** *volunteers in their late teens drawn from schools and colleges throughout Germany.*

The battalions proved to be unmanoeuvrable in action, advancing into their attacks in columns, sometimes singing and with flags flying. They died in droves. For example, when the 2nd Oxfordshire and Buckinghamshire Light Infantry was attacked near Langemarck on 23 October, the student columns advanced to within twenty yards of the British trenches, then turned and marched parallel to them, under fire the whole while. Next morning 720 dead Germans were counted in front of the Oxford and Bucks trenches. There were other similar incidents in the same area, which is why there is a memorial chapel to the *Kindermorde*, the 'Slaughter of the Children', at the entrance of the German Cemetery at Langemarck. Graves in German cemeteries showing a rank of *Kriegsfreiwilliger* (wartime volunteers) mark the burial places of these idealistic but unfortunate young men.

By contrast, Kitchener had insisted that his volunteer battalions serve for up to a year or more before committing them to battle.

A field in Belgium filled with German dead – cut down by the BEF in 1914. German tactics of sending student battalions forward in massed formations resulted in huge casualties at the hands of the professionals.

CHAPTER FIVE

The First Line Territorials

The Territorial Force may have been bypassed by Kitchener in his drive to create the New Army, but the Territorials would be in action before the Kitchener divisions and would ultimately make almost as great a contribution to the British military effort in the war.

The description of the Territorial background can be presented more quickly than the complicated build-up of the various elements in the New Army. The Territorials had been in existence since Haldane brought the Volunteers into the county-regiment system in his 1908 army reforms. They were part-time, volunteer soldiers, trained and ready to become full-time if war came, but only with the commitment to serve as part of Britain's home defence forces. Pre-war Territorial soldiers joined with the obligation to serve for five years. The Territorial Force had an establishment of 417,533 but was 155,700 men short of that figure on the outbreak of war, partly because many of the former Volunteers had decided not to join the new Territorials in 1908 and partly because new men who joined in 1908 allowed their five-year service to lapse in 1913.

'Terriers' of the 5th York and Lancasters, West Riding Division, at their annual summer camp prior to the Great War.

The Territorials were formed into battalions, brigades and divisions, with artillery and other supporting arms, on almost identical lines to units of the Regular Army. There were fourteen divisions in existence in August 1914. No divisional numbers had been issued; they were simply known by the region in which they were formed. Reading from London outwards they were:

> 1st London Division
> 2nd London Division
> Home Counties Division
> Wessex Division
> East Anglian Division
> South Midland Division
> North Midland Division
> Welsh Division
> West Lancashire Division
> East Lancashire Division
> West Riding Division
> Northumbrian Division
> Lowland Division
> Highland Division

There were no Territorials in Ireland.

The 1914 Territorial divisions had professional officers from the Regular Army commanding divisions and brigades and holding staff positions at those levels, and infantry battalions and artillery units

A sergeant-instructor of the 20th Londons (Blackheath and Woolwich) instructs on adjusting the sights of the Long Lee-Enfield rifle.

Pre-war Territorials – Barnsley Company, 5th York and Lancasters, West Riding Division, on weekend musketry training.

usually had a Regular adjutant and Regular NCO instructors. All other officers up to the rank of lieutenant-colonel held Territorial commissions and were usually local business or professional men, with a particularly strong element of solicitors. Although this is mostly an infantry division story, mention should be made of the cavalry element of the Territorials, the Yeomanry. Many of the Yeomanry regiments would fight as infantry in the BEF and at Gallipoli and an infantry division formed from dismounted Yeomanry units later in the war will form part of our *From Six to Sixty-Five* story. There was also a Territorial Force Nursing Service which would mobilize when war came and staff some of the Army's hospitals.

The whole of the Territorial Force was immediately mobilized on the outbreak of war. The 'Terriers' left their civilian homes and lives, reported to their drill halls and became full-time soldiers for at least the duration of the war. The bringing up to strength of the pre-war units and a subsequent expansion into what was known as a 'Second Line' commenced, but Kitchener ordered that the drive for recruiting and the provision of arms and equipment for Territorial expansion was to take second place to the creation of the New Army. Some of the Regular staff officers, adjutants and training NCOs were taken from the Territorial units to help with this formation of New Army units, but the Regular divisional and brigade commanders were usually left in place. Every Territorial soldier was asked if he would be willing to serve overseas and most, over 90 per cent, did so. Units which had a sufficient majority of

Recruiting march for the 24th (County of London) Regiment. The march was twenty miles long from its camp at Tadworth to London. The men are collecting sandwiches during a halt.

such men were then designated as 'General Service' and those units that were short of the required numbers soon recruited enough new volunteers willing to go abroad that it was not long before the entire pre-war Territorial Force was available for duty overseas. Whether this would be to garrison duty in Empire stations or to active service in theatres of war would be the choice of the War Office, the Territorial units having passed out of the juristriction of the County Territorial Associations when the units volunteered for overseas service.

Before moving on to tell how the pre-war Territorials units were employed after the outbreak of war, the individuality of the Territorial Force should be emphasized. The pre-war Regular Army and the New Army were really one, with men and units frequently passing between divisions with one designation or the other. Recruits joining at the county regiment's one depot were sent where needed to Regular or New Army units. The Territorials, however, joined at drill halls which were normally for units of company strength; there could be at least four and up to twenty of these in a county. Territorial recruits trained with Territorial training units. Territorials serving overseas did so in separate divisions. There was a separate base port and camp at Rouen for Territorial units in the BEF. There was a period of emergency in late 1914 and early 1915 when individual Territorial battalions had to be sent out to the BEF and were attached to Regular divisions, but this was only a temporary arrangement and these battalions mostly returned to their own Territorial divisions later. Except for such special

The Inns of Court Volunteers was formed during the reign of George III, and consisted entirely of lawyers. The monarch at the time dubbed them 'The Devil's Own'. I 1908, with the forming of the Territorial Force, it became The Inns of Court Officer Training Corps with the task of training officers for the Territorial Force. During the Great Wa it produced upward. of 12,000 commissioned officers. The two pictures show members during training.

circumstances, all Territorial units preserved their separate identity throughout the war and Territorial officers and soldiers could rely on remaining in those units throughout their period of service. At least in the units of the original fourteen divisions, a unique Territorial spirit would endure throughout.

The Territorials started with many more advantages than the New Army, particularly the fact that commanders, staffs, unit officers and NCOs were normally in place all the way down from the divisional commander to platoon level, and that 60 per cent or more of the men had several years of military training, though admittedly of a part-time nature, behind them. They were certainly more ready for active service than the raw recruits of the New Army to which Kitchener was giving priority.

The Territorials Go Abroad

Territorial units started going overseas at alarming speed. The priority was to replace Regular battalions being withdrawn from key points on the sea route to India, Australia and New Zealand. The first to go were four battalions from the 1st London Division to Malta on 4 September 1914, followed immediately by the 7th and 8th Middlesex, from the Home Counties Division, bound for Gibraltar and then the entire East Lancashire Division to Egypt to protect the Suez Canal. In October the Wessex and the Home Counties Divisions went to India and the Second Line Wessex Division followed in December. There

The 1st/5th York and Lancasters at York prior to them setting off by train on their way to France, March 1915.

were more urgent calls closer to home. The Regular divisions of the BEF were suffering such unexpected casualties in the 1914 battles that there were insufficient reinforcements to replace them. Twenty-three Territorial battalions were sent out and were attached, usually one but sometimes two, to a Regular brigade. The London Scottish were the first in action, at Messines on 31 October. All of these battalions shared the hard fighting and privations of the BEF's Regular units. Six of the battalions came from the 1st London Division, seven from the two Scottish divisions; only five of the twelve Territorial divisions still at home were not called upon to contribute to this temporary depletion of their strengths. (Five Yeomanry regiments also fought as infantry with the BEF at this time – the Oxfordshire Hussars being the first in action, like the London Scottish, at Messines on 31 October – and eight Territorial Royal Engineer field companies were also despatched to the BEF as emergency reinforcements.) Finally, in February 1915, the North Midland Division became the first complete Territorial division to go to an active theatre of war operations when it crossed to France. It would soon be in the line on the Ypres Salient.

All of these movements took place even before the War Office could be concerned with issuing numbers to the Territorial divisions, priority in this being given to the New Army which would not go to war for several months. It was not until May 1915 that divisional numbers were allocated, following on from the last New Army division being formed. Numbers were allocated to the Territorials in the order in which they

The London Scottish marching past Hyde Park on their way to Belgium where they went into action at Messines Ridge on 31 October 1914.

went overseas as complete divisions, starting with the East Lancashire Division which had already been in Egypt for several months defending the Suez Canal.

The First Line Divisions

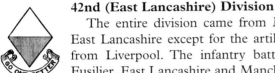

42nd (East Lancashire) Division

The entire division came from Manchester, Salford and towns in East Lancashire except for the artillery howitzer brigade which came from Liverpool. The infantry battalions were from the Lancashire Fusilier, East Lancashire and Manchester Regiments. The division was dispatched to Egypt in September 1914, the first complete Territorial division, as has been said, to go abroad. One wonders, as with the Pals divisions, whether Lord Derby persuaded the War Office to choose Lancashire to provide the senior division in this group. Most of the division provided a defence for the Suez Canal, but one battalion went to Khartoum in the Sudan and half a battalion went to Cyprus.

The division was reassembled in 1915 and sent to Gallipoli, landing at Helles in May and taking part in the Battles of Krithia, trying unsuccessfully to break through the Turkish line across the Helles peninsula in front of Achi Baba hill. After suffering heavy casualties, the division was withdrawn in the last days of December 1915, returning to Egypt to man again the Suez Canal defences throughout 1916.

Gully Ravine, Gallipoli, in September 1915 occupied by men of the 42nd (East Lancashire) Division – the first complete Territorial division to go abroad.

The division was transferred to the Western Front in March 1917 and served there until the Armistice, taking part in the battles of the German March Offensive and the Advance to Victory, concluding a creditable war record for a division which had once thought it might be needed for no more than boring garrison duty in Egypt.

43rd (Wessex) Division

The division drew its infantry from the Devonshire, Somerset Light Infantry, Duke of Cornwall's Light Infantry, Hampshire, Dorsetshire and Wiltshire Regiments.

When the authorities in India allowed the withdrawal of most of the British Regular battalions there, they did so on the understanding that they would be replaced by partially trained Territorial troops. Kitchener's request to the Wessex Division that it take part in this move was accepted and most of the division sailed from Southampton on 9 October 1914, arriving in India in November. When the division sailed for this garrison duty, it left behind the three brigade commanders and their staffs and all the supporting units, except the field artillery, to be employed elsewhere.

The choice of the Wessex Division for this task was almost certainly governed by the proximity of its location to the port of Southampton. At a time when the railway system in England was so hard-pressed with new units being formed and the reinforcement of the BEF taking place, it made sense for the transport ships bringing Regular units from India

The 43rd (Wessex) Division went to India in October 1914 to relieve British Regular battalions for the Western Front. British troops provide guard for Maharaja Jam Saheb of Nawanagar.

to be used by the nearest Territorials to Southampton for the dispatch of their replacements.

It might have seemed that this chance decision would lead to 11,697 Wessex men sailing to a destination which would keep them safe from the hard fighting experienced by most of the other Territorial divisions. A plan was soon made that, once the division had become fully trained in India, it would be transferred to the Western Front and replaced by a Second Line Territorial division; this was not proceeded with because of the German U-boat threat in 1916. But, throughout the war, the division sent men or complete units to reinforce the Allied force fighting in Mesopotamia and in other theatres of war and there were only two of the division's battalions left in India at the Armistice, and only one of these, the 1st/5th Hampshires, had served throughout in India. (The '1st' in front of the pre-war '5th' denotes a First Line Territorial battalion compared to a '2nd' prefix which denotes the Second Line battalions raised during the war; this procedure will be described in detail later.)

44th (Home Counties) Division

The division's infantry came from Middlesex, Surrey and West Kent. The two Middlesex battalions rushed out to garrison Gibraltar in September 1914 never rejoined the division; their places were taken by the 1st Brecknockshire (part of the South Wales Borderers) and the 1st/4th Border.

'Holding the fort' in the far reaches of the British Empire was a job for the Territorial Force. Regulars of the Indian Army were sent to bolster the British forces in Europe.

The (Home Counties) Division was the second division sent to India, sailing only a few days after the Wessex Division and subsequently experiencing similar fortunes to that division, although eight of the battalions which sailed from Southampton were still in India at the end of the war.

(The 45th Division was a Second Line division and will be included in a later section.)

46th (North Midland) Division

The division's units came from Lincolnshire, Leicestershire, Staffordshire, Nottinghamshire and Derbyshire. This was the first complete division to have attained a sufficient level of training to be considered fit for duty on the Western Front. It sailed in February 1915 and held trenches almost continually on the Ypres Salient and Messines Ridge sectors for the next seven months. (It was at the end of this period that my uncle, a platoon sergeant in the 1st/4th Lincolns, died at Poperinghe of wounds received at Sanctuary Wood. Stories from my mother of 'Uncle Andy' sparked my interest in the First World War and led to a career of writing military history and as a battlefield tour operator.)

The division then suffered two misfortunes. It was transferred to the Loos sector in October and hastily thrown against a German strongpoint, the Hohenzollern Redoubt, on the afternoon of 13 October 1915, without having had any opportunity for reconnaissance

The Poperinghe Road out of Ypres and the Salient heavy with traffic in 1915 and an ambulance bringing out the wounded.

or preparation and with no support from any other unit. The disaster when this attack failed with heavy loss was followed in July 1916 when the division again failed in the diversionary attack on the exposed northern flank at Gommecourt on the opening day of the Battle of the Somme. The divisional commander was dismissed and the division seems to have been given the reputation as only being suitable as a 'line-holder'. This situation continued until 29 September 1918 when the division carried out a successful attack, crossing the St Quentin Canal which formed part of the Hindenburg Line defences. The division then continued to take part in the successful advance leading to the Armistice.

47th (2nd London) Division

This was the pre-war 2nd London Division; it obtained its wartime divisional number before that of the 1st London Division only because many of that division's battalions had been sent individually to the Western Front and the division would not be able to reassemble until 1916.

The 47th Division's units were from South-East and South-West London. The infantry were all battalions of the officially all-Territorial London Regiment, but the 1st/22nd and 1st/24th Londons had links with the Regulars of the Queen's (West Surrey) Regiment. Three of the London battalions were known as the Post Office Rifles, the Civil Service Rifles and the London Irish Rifles – pre-war forerunners of the

Men of 235 Brigade, 47th Divisional Artillery, watering horses at Flesquières, 24 November 1917. The division went to France in March 1915 and served successfully to the armistice.

New Army's Pals battalions, I suppose. The 1st/4th Royal Welsh Fusiliers joined as divisional pioneers in 1915.

The division left England in March 1915, destined for a long and successful period of service on the Western Front. It fought at Aubers Ridge, Festubert and Loos in 1915, on the Somme in 1916, capturing High Wood on 15 September and causing its memorial later to be erected there, and in most of the 1917 and 1918 battles, culminating in the triumphal entry into the city of Lille on 28 October 1918.

48th (South Midland) Division

The division's infantry was provided by battalions from the county regiments of Gloucestershire, Worcestershire, Berkshire, Oxford and Buckinghamshire, and a complete brigade from Warwickshire. As with other Territorial divisions, all of the artillery and other supporting units also came from those counties. The 1st/5th Royal Sussex was added in 1915 as the divisional pioneers.

Crossed to France in March 1915 and spent most of the next fifteen months holding trenches, including nearly a year on the northern sector of the Somme front which it took over from French troops in July 1915, being the first British troops to arrive 'on the Somme' and suffering the first British fatal casualty there when Private E. Whitlock of the 1st/4th Oxford and Bucks Light Infantry was killed near Hèbuterne by an early morning shell two days after the takeover from the French (now buried in Gommecourt Wood New Cemetery).

An officer of the 1st/8th Royal Warwicks tries his hand at sniping in the trenches at Hèbuterne, on the Somme, in the summer of 1915.

Two Birmingham battalions – the 1st/6th and 1st/8th Royal Warwicks – were loaned to the Regular 4th Division for the opening day of the Somme in the failed attack on Serre. The South Midland division then carried out five further attacks on the Somme in 1916 and four in Third Ypres in 1917. The division was then transferred to the Italian Front in November 1917 and spent the remainder of the war there, holding trenches and taking part in two set-piece battles, culminating in the pursuit of the defeated Austrian Army in November 1918.

49th (West Riding) Division

The three infantry brigades were provided by the West Yorkshires, the Duke of Wellington's and a brigade shared by the King's Own Yorkshire Light Infantry and the York and Lancasters. The 3rd Monmouths later became the pioneer battalion.

The division crossed to France in April 1915 and served on the Western Front until the Armistice. It faced the first German phosgene gas attack on the Yser Canal sector north of Ypres in December 1915; its divisional memorial now stands on the canal bank above Essex Farm Cemetery which was made famous by the Canadian John McCrae's *In Flanders Fields* poem, written when he was a medical officer working at an aid post dug into the same bank. The division fought on the Somme in 1916, spending a long period on the Thiepval sector, in Third Ypres in 1917 and in the Battles of the Lys and the Advance to Victory in 1918.

Men of the 1st/5th York and Lancs in trenches close to the Yser Canal north of Ypres. Opposing trenches came to within a few yards at this northern point of the whole British-held front.

50th (Northumbrian) Division

The division's units were drawn from Northumberland, Durham and the North and East Ridings of Yorkshire. It crossed to France in April 1915 and had an immediate and traumatic introduction to battle, arriving at a crisis period in the Second Battle of Ypres. Within a week of leaving England, the division's infantry battalions were attached to other divisions fighting to hold ground in the aftermath of the first German chlorine gas attack at Ypres. The division suffered 5,204 casualties, almost all in the infantry, before being withdrawn and concentrating again.

The division served on the Western Front until the Armistice, taking part in the Battles of the Somme in 1916, Arras and Third Ypres in 1917, and in every one of the major battles of 1918.

51st (Highland) Division

The pre-war battalions in the division were all from Highland regiments, but this was the first Territorial division to go to France that had been seriously affected by the earlier sending of individual battalions to support the BEF in 1914 and early 1915. When the division went to France in May 1915 it had 'borrowed' four Lancashire Territorial battalions to bring it up to strength. It was not until early 1916 that the division recovered its lost battalions and became completely Highland again.

The division served on the Western Front until the Armistice, gaining

Gordon Highlanders resting during a route march in 1914. Four battalions of this regiment served in the 51st (Highland) Division.

a fine reputation, particularly for its aggression in attack. It fought on the Somme in 1916, culminating in the capture of the German stronghold of Beaumont-Hamel where the division's fine memorial now stands in the Newfoundland Park. It took part in the Battles of Arras, Third Ypres and Cambrai in 1917, and in all of the big battles of 1918.

52nd (Lowland) Division

The pre-war battalions came from the Glasgow area and the Lowland counties. (The Royal Scots Territorial battalions from the Edinburgh area were in neither of the two pre-war Scottish divisions, but were earmarked for coastal defence, though subsequently all were sent to divisions serving or due to serve overseas.) The Lowland Division lost three battalions to the BEF in 1914 and 1915, replacing them with the 1st/4th and 1st/7th Royal Scots and the 1st/5th Argyll and Sutherland Highlanders just before the division sailed for Egypt in May and June 1915. Before sailing, the train carrying two companies of the 1st/7th Royal Scots was in a collision near Gretna and only sixty-four of the 498 men aboard were not killed or injured, but the battalion was made up with reinforcements and remained with the division.

The division, less the brigade containing the Gretna train-crash battalion which remained in Egypt, landed on the Helles sector at Gallipoli where it was involved in heavy fighting until the evacuation in January 1916. The division fought in the Palestine campaign from April 1916 until March 1918 when it was transferred to the Western Front to

On 22 May, 1915, a troop train carrying two companies of the Royal Scots was in a collision near Gretna resulting in death or injury to 434 men of that battalion.

The wooden coaches burned fiercely and the fire brigades attending were hampered by a lack of water.

In the role-call held shortly after the crash just 52 men answered. Although some had accompanied their injured comrades to hospital.

take part in the Advance to Victory offensives from August to the Armistice, thus concluding a record of honourable involvement in three major theatres of war.

53rd (Welsh) Division

The pre-war division contained two brigades from Wales and one from Cheshire, but it suffered severe depletion when six battalions were sent to reinforce the BEF in the opening months of the war. They never rejoined the division and were mostly replaced with wartime-raised and only partly trained Second Line Territorial battalions from a Home Counties division. This is a good example of the problems encountered by these higher-numbered First Line Territorial divisions which had aided the BEF in this way.

The division sailed for the Mediterranean in July 1915, destined for Gallipoli where it landed at Suvla Bay three days after the first landing there. It served at Suvla for four months, but at the end of November, with heavy casualties from battle, sickness and a blizzard, the infantry was reduced to about one quarter of its normal strength and the division was withdrawn to Egypt.

The division fought in Palestine for the remainder of the war, but its battalions fell so low in strength, due to lack of reinforcements, that it became 'Indianized' in 1918, with only three Welsh battalions (two of them amalgamations) remaining – 5th/6th and 7th Royal Welsh Fusiliers and the 4th/5th Welsh.

Royal Welsh Fusiliers Territorials at their annual camp. Not the most popular of assignments for 'Saturday Night Soldiers' – peeling potatoes for that day's main meal.

54th (East Anglian) Division

The pre-war division came from Essex, Suffolk, Norfolk, Bedfordshire, Northamptonshire, Cambridgeshire and Hertfordshire. After losing the only Cambridgeshire and Hertfordshire battalions and one of the Suffolk battalions to the BEF, replacements came in the form of the 1st/10th and 1st/11th Londons (from Hackney and Pentonville) and the 1st/8th Hampshires (the Isle of Wight Rifles).

The war service of this division was almost identical to that of the 53rd (Welsh), landing at Suvla Bay one day after the Welsh, and then going on to fight in Palestine for the remainder of the war, though the division managed to maintain its strength and every one of the battalions which went overseas in July 1915 was present at the end.

55th (West Lancashire) Division

The pre-war infantry were six battalions of the King's (Liverpool) and two each of the King's Own Royal Lancasters (from Ulverston and Lancaster), the South Lancashires (Warrington and St Helens) and the Loyal North Lancashires (Preston and Bolton), but these were all dispersed in 1914-15, with nine battalions being sent to the BEF and three to enable the 51st (Highland) Division to proceed at full strength to France. It was not until January 1916 that the division was able to reform, in France, with all of the original infantry returning and the 1st/4th South Lancashires (from Warrington) being added as divisional pioneers.

Double Victoria Cross winner Noel Chavasse with his stretcher bearers – 1st/10th King's Liverpool Regiment (Liverpool Scottish).

The first divisional action was at Guillemont, on the Somme, in August 1916, the action in which Captain Noel Chavasse, Medical Officer of the 1st/10th King's (the Liverpool Scottish), won the first of his two Victoria Crosses. In 1917 the division took part in the Battles of Third Ypres and Cambrai, and in 1918 in those of the Lys and the Advance to Victory. The division has a fine memorial in the village of Givenchy-lès-la-Bassée where the division stood firm there and at nearby Festubert on the southern hinge of the German offensive on the Lys in April 1918.

56th (1st London) Division

The numbering of this division should be explained. Before the war it had been the 1st London Division, the senior of London's two Territorial divisions, but the extensive use of its pre-war battalions to provide overseas garrisons, reinforcements for the BEF and to make up other divisions' shortages in 1914 and 1915 caused it to be the last of the pre-war Territorials to be concentrated into a complete division in France in February 1916. The pre-war artillery, engineers and medical units had also been dispersed. Only the original artillery and seven of the original infantry battalions rejoined their old division, but the replacements for the lost units all came from London, although the battalion sent as divisional pioneers was the 1st/5th Cheshires, originally part of the pre-war Welsh Division.

The reborn division fought its first battle on the opening day of the Somme in 1916, capturing most of its objectives in the diversionary attack at Gommecourt, but having to pull back to its original line when the other division taking part in the diversion failed. The Londons fought again on the Somme, at Arras, Third Ypres and Cambrai in 1917, and in most of the 1918 battles up to the Armistice.

Men of the London Scottish, out of the line, 2 April 1918. They are enjoying a period of 'rest' and training digging trenches at Mont St Eloi.

CHAPTER SIX

The Second Line Territorials

A majority of pre-war Territorials in every unit had volunteered for overseas service in the days following the outbreak of war, but individual members of those units had not all so volunteered and were left behind when the units departed for the divisional concentration areas well away from their home localities. Such men would continue to be classified as 'Home Service' men and would retain their right not to be sent overseas throughout the war. The War Office decided that the men left behind should remain on full-time duty at the local drill halls and start forming reserve units to train the wartime volunteers coming in to the Territorials. So, every Territorial unit that had gone away had a new unit being formed in its wake. This became the 'Second Line', the 'First Line' being the original unit then preparing for overseas service. The prefixes '1st/' and '2nd/' differentiated the two levels, hence the 1st/4th Lincolns for my uncle's battalion then at Luton preparing to go to France and the 2nd/4th Lincolns for the new unit forming at Boston and the other South Lincolnshire drill halls. Wartime volunteers had no 'Home Service' right and could expect to be sent abroad, indeed

July 1915 – the Bishop of London, Arthur Winnington-Ingram, preaches a sermon of hate to **London Territorials on the steps of St Paul's: '...everyone that puts principle above ease, and life itself beyond mere living, are banded in a great crusade – we can not deny it – to kill Germans: to kill them not for the sake of killing, but to save the world; to kill the good as well as the bad, to kill the young men as well as the old, to kill those who have shown kindness to our wounded... to kill them lest the civilization of the world should itself be killed.'**

that is what most joined up for.

The War Office was not initially pushing forward this Second Line expansion with any urgency; the main effort was devoted to the creation of the New Army. The Second Line's role was initially envisaged as being no more than providing reinforcements for the First Line and it was not until well into 1915 that the War Office allowed Second Line units to recruit up to full strength and the process of forming complete Second Line Territorial divisions to commence. Divisional numbers were issued in August 1915. (These notes will not apply to the Second Line Wessex Division which received special treatment.)

Although the War Office was not encouraging Territorial recruitment, men started to apply at drill halls in large numbers as soon as the war started. The Territorial Force, 155,700 men short of its pre-war establishment on the outbreak of war, was 90,000 men over that figure by the end of October 1914! There were several reasons why the Territorials did so well rather than suffer from the competition of what might be seen as the more glamorous New Army. First, the men who had signed on for the five-year commitment in 1908 and allowed that to lapse in 1913 came back almost to a man. Second, men who had brothers or other relatives in the pre-war Territorials enlisted in the hope of serving with them. A less obvious third source of recruits was to be found in men of marginal physical standard who just failed the examination at the Regular Army recruiting offices; the Territorial doctors were more likely to turn a blind eye to minor defects. Finally,

Lighter side of military training, the start of the 'camel' race in the regimental sports in the Second Line battalion of the London Irish.

there were parts of the country that were strongly Territorially minded. London was the foremost of these; 450,000 Londoners served in the Territorials during the war, one seventh of the total Territorial wartime manpower. Some of the more rural counties were also strong supporters, the euphoria of the Pals movement in the big cities not affecting such areas. Conversely, it will be seen in the listing of the Second Line divisions that some industrial areas, such as the North-East, would find it difficult to keep their Second Line up to strength. Scotland would suffer in the same way because its population was insufficient to replace the heavy casualties to its Regular and New Army units at Loos and on the Somme as well as sustaining its First Line Territorials.

Men there were aplenty in most places, but not commanders, staffs and officers. The Second Line divisions had to compete with the New Army for divisional and brigade commanders and staffs, and infantry battalions and other units had to make do with the few pre-war officers and NCOs who had refused to volunteer for or were unfit for overseas service. Such men stayed in Britain and were often quickly promoted. The Territorial equivalent of 'dug-out' officers, often not having served since the pre-1908 days of the Volunteers, were welcomed back as middle-ranking officers and many a young local man of the right social class was granted an instant commission as a subaltern. In the city areas, however, the rush of the ex-public schoolboys and the middle-class clerical classes into the Pals battalions left the Second Line

Soldier-making at express speed – according to **The Illustrated War News** *22 September 1915. Forty-five minutes after enlisting these men are being instructed on the 18-pounder.*

Territorials short of junior officer and NCO material.

The Second Line divisions duly formed, exact shadows of the First Line, their numbering following on from the 56th (1st London) Division, the last formed of the First Line, although the Second Line divisions did not form in the same order as the First Line. They were intended for eventual overseas service, but, with the exception of Wessex's Second Line division which was a special case, their primary duty throughout 1915 was to continue training the wartime Territorial volunteers as reinforcements for their First Line equivalents. This resulted in the first of the Second Line divisions not reaching an active front until May 1916. All escaped the Somme and half of the Second Line divisions would never see a fighting front. Those that did represented virtually the end of Kitchener's build-up of a large fighting force of divisions and were sometimes looked down upon by senior commanders on the Western Front. But, considering the difficulties under which they had been formed, particularly the sending of so many of their best men to reinforce the First Line, those Second Line divisions that did reach the fighting behaved creditably.

There is one more step that should be described. Whenever a Second Line unit proceeded abroad, it once again left its Home Service men behind. To the pre-war Territorials who had refused to go abroad were now added the many lower medical category men – often semi-recovered wounded from the First Line. These were formed into a Third Line, so to the 1st/4th and 2nd/4th Lincolns, for example, was

Third Line Territorials – NCOs of the 3rd/5th City of London Regiment (London Rifle Brigade) in the summer of 1915. Third Line battalions were formed when the Second Line were sent to the front.

now added the 3rd/4th Lincolns. Once again the pre-war Territorials who still insisted on being Home Service had the opportunity of being promoted. Such men were few in number and most had good family reasons for not going when so many of their pre-war comrades had gone abroad, with many becoming casualties by now, but some had no good reason and would later bear the stigma of being slackers. I can speak with personal family knowledge of such a situation in a community.

The Third Line units were never formed into divisions and never went abroad, but remained purely as reserve units performing the dual functions of training fit men for the First and Second Line and of holding lower-category men as home-defence units, usually at a coastal location. In January 1916, with conscription looming, the Army stopped specific volunteering for the Territorials and it was not long before the Third Line dropped the '3rd/' prefix and simply became 'Reserve Battalions' of the Territorial Force. This was the beginning of the weakening of that unique Territorial voluntary spirit and identity which had existed long before Kitchener started to form his New Army.

Let us see what became of those fourteen Second Line divisions.

45th (2nd Wessex) Division

The history of this division is unusual. We go back to 1914 when the War Office hurriedly dispatched the pre-war Territorial Wessex and Home Counties Divisions to India as garrison troops to replace the Regular units brought home. In November 1914 the pre-war Welsh

Territorial units in training: men of the 2nd/15th Battalion The London Regiment (Prince of Wales' Own Civil Service Rifles). Clearing a trench with the bayonet and cyclists acting as scouts communicating by telephone.

Territorial Division was warned for a similar duty, but this plan was dropped; perhaps Lloyd George urged a more active role for that division. To provide the third division required for India, the War Office made the surprising decision to send the Second Line Wessex Territorial Division, made up of units which must have been almost exclusively composed of wartime volunteers with only a few weeks service. Once again, a factor in this decision must have been the proximity of the Wessex units to the port of Southampton, allowing the units to embark on the troopships bringing men back from India and the Far East without placing too much strain on Britain's railway system. The preparation of the division for this unexpected duty proceeded apace. The decision to send the division was taken on 30 November; it sailed on 12 December. Only ten of its twelve battalions and nine of its eleven field artillery batteries were ready. The 2nd/6th Hampshires and the 2nd/5th Devons were the battalions left behind; they never rejoined. I find this rapid embarkation of nearly 10,000 raw troops almost breathtaking. At a time when the War Office was giving priority in recruitment and equipment to the New Army, an exception must have been made for Wessex. This was helped by the fact that no Southern Division was being formed for the New Army. Of the six county regiments classed as Wessex for Territorial purposes, two – Somerset and Cornwall - were Light Infantry whose New Army units went to the Light Division in the New Army and the Wiltshires went to the Western Division. That left Devon, Dorset and Hampshire as 'orphan counties'

Territorials of The London Regiment marching in India during the war. Territorial units served in India and the Middle East.

whose men were not so urgently needed in the New Army and made it easier for their Territorial battalions to recruit their Second Line. The ten Second Line Wessex battalions which went to India did so with only 830 men each, compared with the 1,000 men in a normal battalion; the artillery batteries went with 145 men each instead of the normal 198. Medical and engineer units were never even raised. Although it was a Second Line division, the 2nd Wessex was given the divisional number of 45 – fourth in the First Line list of numbering and ahead of most of the First Line divisions.

It should not be thought that the Wessex men settled down to a danger-free four years in India while other divisions suffered the heat of battle elsewhere. Seven of the ten battalions were later transferred to various fighting fronts, two of them, the 2nd/4th Somerset Light Infantry and the 2nd/4th Hampshires, finishing up on the Western Front. Only three battalions – the 2nd/5th Somerset Light Infantry, 2nd/4th Duke of Cornwall's Light Infantry and 2nd/4th Wiltshires – of the division's infantry were left in India at the war's end and all of the artillery had also been sent away as reinforcements or had been dispersed.

(Most of the infantry in the remaining divisions of this group were the Second Line of the pre-war Territorial battalions in the corresponding First Line divisions. For this reason, details of the county origins of the Second Line battalions will not be repeated unless of particular interest.)

An artery of the British Empire – the Suez Canal. This important waterway required to be defended against Turkish attack.

57th (2nd West Lancashire) Division

For the third time a Lancashire division comes first in the numbering of a major group of divisions, even though four other Second Line divisions went to France before the 57th.

The division crossed to France in February 1917 and fought its first battle on the northernmost sector of Third Ypres in October-November. It was fortunate in missing the German 1918 offensives and took part in the successful attacks of the Advance to Victory period in August to October.

58th (2nd/1st London) Division

The '2nd/1st' means that this was the Second Line of the pre-war 1st London Division.

A brigade consisting of the four most senior battalions – the 2nd/1st to 2nd/4th Londons - had a tough and unusual experience. In late 1914 and early 1915 they were sent, with their brigade headquarters, to Malta to relieve their First Line equivalents who had gone there in the opening weeks of the war but had since been sent to reinforce the BEF. In August 1915 the four Second Line battalions left Malta and in October and September were landed at the Helles and Suvla sectors at Gallipoli and attached to various divisions there. At the end of that campaign they returned to Egypt and in March 1916 were transferred to France. But they were not required in France in their weakened state and, sadly, were disbanded and their men transferred to other London

Entrance to the Grand Harbour, Malta. An important military station for operations in the Mediterranean that had to be garrisoned, for the most part by Territorial units.

battalions. Their places in the 58th Division, to which they had belonged for such a short time, had meanwhile been taken by their equivalent Third Line battalions, the 3rd/1st to 3rd/4th Londons, these probably becoming the only Third Line Territorial battalions to see active service.

The main division crossed to France in January 1917, fought with the Australians at Bullecourt in May and then played a prominent part in Third Ypres. In March 1918 the division found itself at the southern extremity of the BEF line, on the Somme next to the French, when the Germans struck on the first day of their offensive, creating a gap between the Londons and the main BEF front. For the next two weeks the division fought under French command until it could return to the BEF. It survived in good heart to take part in the opening day of the great Allied offensive on 8 August, its well-known rider and injured horse memorial now being in the village of Chipilly which it captured the following day. The inscription on the memorial refers to that action being the start of the German retreat which culminated in the Armistice on 11 November. The 58th Division was in the advancing line when the ceasefire brought fighting to an end that day.

59th (2nd North Midland) Division

This division formed without difficulty in early 1915. Following the Easter Rising in Dublin in April 1916, the entire division was sent to Ireland to restore order, English troops being required for this task

With the rebellion in Ireland, beginning Easter Monday 24 April 1916, the 59th Division was shipped out to help maintain order. Here a group of Territorials on the streets of Dublin enjoy a break shortly after having had a brush with the rebels.

rather than Irish units. The division remained in Ireland, continuing its training and sending reinforcements to its First Line in the BEF until returning to England in January 1917 and then crossing to France in February.

The 6th/7th Royal Scots Fusiliers, a battalion amalgamated in the 15th (Scottish) Division reorganization after the Battle of Loos, joined in France as the divisional pioneers.

The division fought in Third Ypres and at Cambrai in 1917, but in March 1918 had the misfortune to be hit hard by the German offensive on the Somme and, then again in April, on the Lys. Casualties were so heavy that the division ceased to exist as a fighting force. The battalions were mostly disbanded, the surviving men usually being sent to sister battalions in the 46th (North Midland) Division. The 59th Division was made up again with new battalions sent from all over Britain and fought again in August and November, but it was no longer a North Midland division.

60th (2nd/2nd London) Division

This was the Second Line of the pre-war 2nd London Division.

Because of problems following London battalions being sent out to support the BEF in 1914 and early 1915, three of the infantry battalions were not exact 'sisters' of their First Line battalions in the 47th Division, but all of the infantry came from that rich source of Territorial supply, the London Regiment. The pioneer battalion added

British troops entering Jerusalem in November 1917. General Edmund Allenby brought off a well designed attack in October and broke through to the city. The 60th Division were involved.

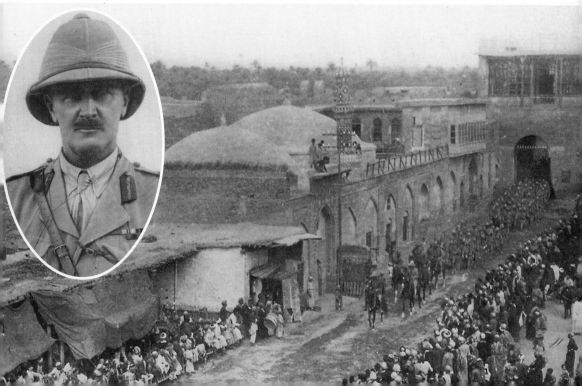

in 1916 was the 1st/12th Loyal North Lancashires. The division crossed to France in June 1916 but was required to do no more than trench-holding on various sectors of the Western Front until the end of 1916 when it began a series of important moves.

The first of these was to Salonika where it was in action in April and May 1917, but then it moved again, in June, to Egypt to prepare for what would be a prolonged and arduous participation in the campaign to clear the Turks out of Palestine and which included taking part in the capture of Jerusalem in December 1917. In mid-1918 the division was 'Indianized'. Seven of the London battalions moved to France and two were disbanded, all being replaced by Indian battalions. Only the 2nd/13th, 2nd/19th and 2nd/22nd Londons remained to keep this at least a partially London division to the end of the war. Those three battalions came from Kensington, St Pancras and Bermondsey respectively.

61st (2nd South Midland) Division

This division formed without difficulty and became the first Second Line division to proceed to a fighting front when it sailed for France in May 1916. It was soon in major action when it was chosen to take part, with the 5th Australian Division, in an attack at Fromelles which was supposed to attract a diversion of German reserves from the British offensive raging on the Somme. The action was a costly failure which made no impression on German dispositions. The South Midland

Fromelles where the 61st Division attacked along with the 5th Australian Division. Picture left shows Australians about to go over the top. After the attack the Germans are seen re-occupying their Second Line after the Australians had withdrawn because the 61st men had failed to take their objectives.

battalions failed to get into the German trenches, much to the anger of the Australians who did succeed but were then left with an open flank. Fromelles was seen in retrospect as an action that should never have taken place.

The division remained on the Western Front until the Armistice, fighting in Third Ypres and at Cambrai in 1917, and in all of the major battles of 1918, showing that Second Line Territorials could make a significant contribution to the BEF's operations.

62nd (2nd West Riding) Division

This division also formed without difficulty and crossed to France in January 1917. It went into the line on the Ancre sector of the Somme on 15 February and a Leeds soldier, Rifleman C.E. Ward, became the first man in the division to die on active service when he was hit that day. I mention this because he is buried in a beautiful little local cemetery, Ten Tree Alley Cemetery, near Serre.

It was not long before the division was flung into bloody attacks at Bullecourt in April and May, which so weakened the division that it was not chosen for battle again until the attack at Cambrai with the tanks in November, a task which it performed successfully. The division's memorial is at Havrincourt on the Cambrai battlefield. The division lost six of its West Riding battalions disbanded or transferred in the February 1918 shake-up of divisions and took in three stranger battalions, the 2nd/20th Londons and two battalions – the 1st/5th

The Battle of Cambrai was the action where the 62nd (West Riding) Division first fought with some real success. A tank rumbles past some soldiers at rest and fails to draw their attention.

Devons and 2nd/4th Hampshires – which had gone to India with the two Wessex divisions in 1914.

The reorganized division experienced much hard fighting in 1918, facing German offensives on the Somme in March and then, in a supposedly quiet rest sector on the French front, in July. The division survived these trials and took part in successful attacks from August right through to the final victory in November, another division bringing credit to the Second Line Territorials.

63rd (2nd Northumbrian) Division

We are now reaching Second Line divisions which experienced difficulty in maintaining their strengths. Northumbria – Northumberland, Durham and the North and East Ridings of Yorkshire for the purposes of this division – formed its Second Line division in the normal manner, but the heavy demands for reinforcements from its First Line division – the 50th, which had been flung piecemeal into the Second Battle of Ypres on its arrival in France in April 1915 – could not be made up by a male population which was also expected to maintain its Regulars and the New Army units raised in the first flush of recruiting enthusiasm in 1914, as well as keeping the coal mines and industry of the North-East working for the war effort.

In July 1916 the War Office decided to break up the division. The units did not disappear, however, all were transferred to useful duty elsewhere. Eight battalions were sent to help form three new Home

Although more and more women were being used to work at jobs normally reserved for men in the North-East, coalmining, shipbuilding and other heavy industry remained the preserve of men and intakes into the Army in this region suffered as a consequence.

Defence divisions; the 2nd/7th Northumberland Fusiliers went to
Egypt and the 2nd/4th East Yorks to Bermuda, both for garrison duty;
and the 2nd/5th and 2nd/9th Durham Light Infantry went to the
Salonika Front. The divisional artillery went to the BEF to become part
of the reorganized Royal Naval Division; the engineers went to
Mesopotamia and the medical units to Salonika. Six of the battalions
which went to the Home Defence divisions disappeared when those
divisions were disbanded in 1918, but the 2nd/6th Durham Light
Infantry went to the BEF and the 2nd/7th took part in the North
Russia Expedition in 1919. No other division saw its original units
dispersed so widely.

It was the disbandment of this division in 1916 which enabled its
number, 63rd, to be allocated to the Royal Naval Division, newly
arrived in France and coming fully under Army control. It was a happy
coincidence that part of the Northumbrian spirit served on in the new
63rd Division when the former division's artillery was transferred to it.
Further Northumbrian links were to be found in the survivors of those
North-East New Army recruits who had been transferred to the Naval
Division on its formation in 1914 and their friends at home who
volunteered to join them in division later (see pages 35 and 37).

64th (2nd Highland) Division

Scotland was another area whose population could not replace its
early casualties, particularly those at Loos in 1915, as well as maintain

*Following the German bombardment of resorts on the East Coast on 16 December 1914, the
manning of coastline defences took on more importance. Training battalions provided the
necessary defences.*

all of its units. All Scottish units, Regular, New Army and Territorial, would be short of reinforcements in the second half of the war.

This division was formed in January 1915 with a completely Highland content, but it became so understrength that the War Office designated it as 'Home Defence' and it moved to Norfolk for that role in 1916. In 1917 all twelve Highland battalions were disbanded and, although the 64th Division remained active in Norfolk until the end of the war, it was no longer a Highland unit.

65th (2nd Lowland) Division

This division suffered difficulties in forming and there was some rearrangement of battalions before it moved to England to become a Home Defence division in Essex in March 1916, but still with a completely Lowland content. In January 1917 the division moved to Ireland for garrison duties, but the men it sent as reinforcements to the First Line Lowland Division could not be replaced in sufficient numbers and the War Office decided to disband the division in early 1918.

66th (2nd East Lancashire) Division

This division formed without difficulty in 1914, but its requirement to provide reinforcements for its First Line sister division, the 42nd, at Gallipoli, meant that it was not ready for overseas service until March 1917 when it crossed to France, the last Second Line Territorial

Scarborough, Whitby and Hartlepool were attacked by the **Seydlitz, Moltke, Van der Tann, Derflinger** *and* **Blücher.**
Houses in Cleveland Road, Hartlepool wrecked by shells. In the Teesside port 420 civilians and soldiers were killed and injured.

One of the East Coast raiders the German battle-cruiser **Moltke.**

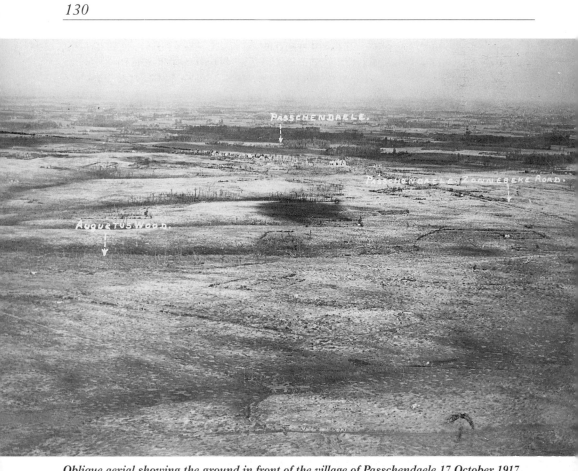

PASSCHENDAELE.

PASSCHENDAELE ZONNEBEKE ROAD.

AUGUSTUS WOOD.

Oblique aerial showing the ground in front of the village of Passchendaele 17 October 1917. Smashed up terrain and two captured German bunkers in the Salient, 1917.

division to proceed on active service.

The division fought well in the Third Battle of Ypres in October 1917. In its attack on 9 October, a small group of Lancashire Fusiliers managed to enter the ruins of Passchendaele village, the first British troops to do so, but their presence could not be reinforced and they had to withdraw. Passchendaele was not captured until a month later. The division now has a beautiful memorial window in the church at Passchendaele, showing the coats of arms of Manchester and the neighbouring towns which provided the division's units.

The division suffered such severe casualties when engulfed by the German March offensive in 1918 that it ceased to exist as a fighting force. All but two of its battalions were disbanded or dispersed; only the 6th Lancashire Fusiliers and the 9th Manchesters remained in the reconstituted division which took part in the Advance to Victory battles. Surprise elements of the division in those final months were the presence of the South African Brigade which was transferred from the 9th (Scottish) Division in September 1918 and three Irish battalions transferred from the 10th (Irish) Division which had been fighting in Palestine but had then been turned into an Indian division.

67th (2nd Home Counties) Division

This division formed in the normal way and was ready for overseas service in 1916. Twice it was warned to be ready to proceed to Ireland and once to France, but all moves were cancelled. Five of its original

Slaving over hot pans – Welsh Territorial army cooks prepare a meal.

battalions were posted away in 1915, three to become part of the 53rd (Welsh) Division which went to Gallipoli and Palestine, and two going to Egypt. All were replaced by their Third Line sister battalions. Three further battalions were sent to France in 1916. In 1917 all remaining Home Counties battalions were disbanded to provide reinforcements elsewhere and the division ceased to be a Territorial one. The reconstituted division, with battalions from a variety of sources, remained in East Anglia on Home Defence duty until the end of the war.

68th (2nd Welsh) Division

This division formed normally, but started losing battalions disbanding through lack of numbers from 1915 onwards until, like the 67th Division, the Territorial battalions all disappeared in late 1917, the reconstituted division remaining on Home Defence duties in Suffolk.

69th (2nd East Anglian) Division

This division underwent the same experiences as the 68th Division, although its Home Defence locations were in the North of England.

We have now catalogued seventy-one 1914-18 infantry divisions, of which sixty-three experienced active service conditions during the war.

Recruiting meeting held in Trafalgar Square and the means to move men in the crowd to join up – a picture of Edith Cavell shot by the Germans in Belgium for assisting British soldiers to evade capture.

CHAPTER SEVEN

A Changing Army

The story so far is of the British Army's Regular divisions being sent to war, followed by the raising of a host of new divisions created out of wartime volunteers of various kinds. But, as the war moved on through 1916, the character of all these divisions changed. The flow of volunteers had slackened and almost ceased in 1915. There had been enough new men so far to replace the Regulars' casualties and to complete the thirty New Army divisions and the First Line Territorials, but, as we have seen, not sufficient to complete the Second Line Territorial group of divisions. The Regulars, First Line Territorials and the New Army went into the Somme offensive at full strength on 1 July 1916 and fought on for 140 days alongside a French Army weakened by Verdun. But the attempt to force a decision in 1916 failed, although the Somme did contribute to the weakening by attrition of the German Army. Kitchener did not live to see what happened to his magnificent creation on the Somme; he was drowned three weeks before the battle started while on passage to meetings in Russia.

'Sign of the times' women bill-stickers putting up a poster reminding men that compulsory service is about to be introduced.   The last appearance of Lord Kitchener in London, 2 June 1916.

Conscription

The BEF suffered 643,249 casualties in 1916, about 85 per cent of them in British units, the remainder in Empire contingents. Such losses could no longer be replaced with volunteers. A shortage had been foreseen at the start of the year, though not as deep a need as the Somme casualty lists would produce. The drastic step of conscription was decided upon in January 1916 and the first single men between the ages of eighteen and forty-one were called up in March, to be followed by married men a few weeks later. The call-ups of men reaching the ages of eighteen would continue until the end of the war. Conscription was not extended to Ireland, the British Government being unwilling to force men to train as soldiers whose loyalty might be doubtful and who might even become enemies after the war.

Approximately 7,550,000 men in Britain came into the eighteen to forty-one age group during the war. That overall total falls neatly into three nearly equal groups:

2,532,684 (33.6 per cent) volunteered in 1914-15,

2,438,218 (32.3 per cent) were conscripted in 1916-18,

2,576,664 (34.1 per cent) were medically unfit or were granted exemption from call-up.★

★ The figures come from *Statistics of the Military Effort of the British Empire during the Great War*, HMSO 1922, pages 364-8. The main exemption groups were: munitions and shipbuilding – 1,032,181; mining – 502,709; railway and transport – 401,641; agriculture – 340,506. This publication will be referred to simply as *Statistics of the Military Effort* in future footnotes.

Some of the first of the conscripts reporting themselves at the Central Recruiting Office, London, January 1916.

The high figure of exemptions was a disappointment to the Army because the number of conscripts was not proving sufficient to replace casualties. The BEF would be 150,000 infantry below strength at the end of 1916. The struggle to maintain divisions would now be a greater task than that of their creation.

(The British Government requested the white Dominions to apply conscription to their male populations in 1916. New Zealand agreed at once. Canada did so in 1917, but was so slow in its implementation that it had little effect upon the Canadian contribution. In Australia, however, conscription became the cause of fierce debate. Prime Minister Billy Hughes made it the main issue of a General Election in September 1916, but the opinions of the Australian soliders already serving, that they did not wish to share their trenches with pressed men, persuaded their families back home to vote against Hughes and he lost the election. The subject was never introduced again in Australia during the war. The results of these various responses can be see in the proportions of the respective estimated male populations who served abroad or who were under training for overseas service at the end of the war: New Zealand – 19.35 per cent, Canada – 13.48 per cent, Australia – 13.43 per cent.*)

* Ibid, page 363.

Tribunal at Fulham Town Hall hearing an application for postponement. Presiding is Lieutenant Norris, Mayor of Fulham.

The effect of conscription in the British divisions was to produce a weakening of the distinctions between what had once been purely Regular, New Army and Territorial. Volunteering for the Territorials was stopped when conscription was introduced. Henceforth, new reinforcements for all divisions, as opposed to their returning wounded and sick, would be conscripts. The first to feel the change were the Second Line Territorials. All through 1916, while their divisions were trying to build up their strengths preparatory to embarking for active service, they had been sending their best men as drafts of reinforcements to their First Line equivalents on the various war fronts. The resulting shortages were now made up with conscripts. When seven of the Second Line divisions eventually went to the BEF, they were referred to, somewhat derisively, as 'conscript divisions' because of their high proportion of such men. It was a term that could eventually be extended to every division on active service.

Another practice to be stopped in early 1916 was the direct commissioning of junior officers. Special Officer Cadet Battalions were formed in Britain to which were sent the young men still coming into the Army from civilian life who had been at public school or in university Officer Training Corps and the many good men already in the Army who had experience of active service and were recommended

Conscripts marching off to the railway station behind a brass band. With conscription the character of the Army was changing.

by their unit commanders. After successful completion of a four-month course, such men were commissioned and would provide the junior officer reinforcements for the remainder of the war. A total of 107,929 men were commissioned in this way at the twenty-three Officer Cadet Battalions which were formed.

More New Divisions

In late 1916 the War Office decided to form some of the many reserve units now in Britain into three new divisions organized on an operational basis but required only for home defence. Each of the three divisions was provided with a brigade of three battalions from the broken-up 63rd (2nd Northumbrian) Division and two brigades, again of three battalions each, of various types of reserve units in England. There were also artillery, engineer and medical units as in normal infantry divisons, but not pioneer, machine-gun or trench-mortar units. With five Second Line Territorial divisions also at home because they could not attain full strength and go overseas, that would make eight divisions carrying out home defence duties. It was in those divisions that Lloyd George, as Prime Minister in 1917-18, was accused of concealing thousands of fit, trained men, keeping the BEF short of such men in his attempt to restrict Haig's ability to mount costly offensives. The three new Home Service divisions – the 71st, 72nd and 73rd – should be included in our cataloguing of the wartime expansion of divisions. (A projected 70th Division was never formed.)

Lloyd George inspecting the brigade based at Llandudno, North Wales. He was accused of concealing thousands of fit, trained men in an attempt to curb Haig's costly offensives.

71st Division

The division was formed in Hampshire and Surrey in November 1916. The brigade from the Second Line Northumbrian Division was all from the Durham Light Infantry. The six other battalions came from London, East Anglia and Southern England. The medical units were from Wales and the engineers from Lancashire and Scotland. There would, however, be much rearrangement of these units during the following year. The division moved to Essex in March 1917, with headquarters at Colchester and with the responsibility of defending the local coastline. In December of 1917 it was decided to break up the three divisions in this series and, by April 1918, the 71st Division ceased to exist.

72nd Division

The division was formed in Somerset in November 1916. The infantry consisted of a Northumberland Fusilier brigade and six other varied battalions. The engineers were mostly from Glamorgan and the medical units from the South Midlands. The division moved to Bedfordshire and Northamptonshire in January 1917, and then, in May, to Essex for coastal defence, where it remained until the division was broken up in early 1918.

Captured Turkish guns and transport in Palestine. Forces that had successfully defended the Suez Canal went on to the offensive. General Sir Archibald Murray managed to form two divisions from troops already in Egypt to help with the push for Palestine.

73rd Division

The division was formed at Blackpool in November 1916. The infantry were a Green Howards brigade from the Northumbrian Division, five Lancashire battalions and the 8th Dorsets. The engineers were from Kent and East Lancashire and the medical units from the Home Counties. The division moved to Essex and Hertfordshire in January 1917 and remained there until broken up in early 1918.

There remain just two more new divisions to be listed, though they were formed mainly from existing units, not fresh ones.

In early 1917 it was decided that the forces which had successfully defended the Suez Canal should go on the offensive and advance into Turkish-held Palestine. The British commander in Egypt, General Sir Archibald Murray, who was in command of this operation, decided that he could produce two further infantry divisions from various sources, to add to those already at his disposal. The War Office agreed, no troops needing to be diverted from other active theatres. The two new divisions were thus formed and played prominent parts in a campaign that would eventually lead to the defeat of Turkey and an end of its huge empire.

74th (Yeomanry) Division

Yeomanry were the cavalry component of the Territorial Force. After their pre-war members had volunteered to serve overseas, thirty-eight Yeomanry regiments were sent to the Mediterranean, where most of

Turkish prisoners being escorted by British troops through the streets of Baghdad.

them fought as infantry in the Anzac and Suvla sectors at Gallipoli before being withdrawn to Egypt. Three Yeomanry brigades, still dismounted, were formed in Egypt and it was these brigades which were then formed into this new division in March 1917. The division was organized on a standard infantry basis but the term 'Yeomanry' was incorporated into the division's title and its Yeomanry spirit and tradition would always remain.

Eighteen Yeomanry regiments, many understrength after Gallipoli, were transformed into twelve infantry battalions which then became parts of their most appropriate infantry county regiments. Ten of the battalions were from England, five from Wales and three from Scotland. Most of the engineer and medical units were also provided by the Yeomanry, the engineers being mostly Welsh, but the division's artillery came from a variety of sources.

The division fought in Palestine for a year, taking part in the Battles of Gaza and Beersheba and in the capture of Jerusalem in December 1917. But, following the disasters in France when the Germans pushed back Gough's Fifth Army in the March 1918 offensive, the division was surprised to receive orders to transfer to the Western Front. It reached France in May, still acting as an infantry division, and took part in the successful series of attacks from September onwards and was in the

German rearguard waits for the appearance over the skyline of pursuing British soldiers during the Advance to Victory, beginning August 1918.

Correction

See page 140, lines 10-12; sentence should read:

" Ten of the distinguished Yeomanry regiments were English, five were Welsh and three were Scottish. "

advancing line when the Armistice came into effect on 11 November.

Although this division had an active service life of less than two years, the earlier fighting of many of its men at Gallipoli gave them a war record as long as many of the earlier established divisions.

75th Division

The second division formed in Egypt did so by taking four battalions of an Indian brigade defending the Suez Canal and eight battalions from the two Wessex Territorial divisions which had been sent to carry out garrison duties in India in 1914. The artillery came from various sources, but included three South African batteries. Most of the engineers were Kent Territorials. The medical units were a mixture, but were partly Indian at one stage.

The division took from April to October of 1917 to fully assemble, but it then went into action in Palestine where it experienced twelve months of campaigning.

A new division was formed in Egypt from British troops sent out to India on garrison duties and Indian battalions. Here British troops try out the novelty of camel riding.

This concludes the listing of British Army infantry divisions of the First World War. Starting from the six pre-war divisions which went to the BEF on the outbreak of war, the Army made the startling expansion to seventy-six infantry divisions:

Regulars	11
Guards	1
Royal Naval (63rd Division)	1
New Army (mostly Army raised)	19
New Army (mostly locally raised)	11
First Line Territorials	14
Second Line Territorials	14
Home Service	3
Yeomanry (74th Division)	1
Raised in Egypt (75th Division)	1

65
65

Sixty-five of these divisions served on active fighting fronts, hence my *From Six to Sixty-Five* story.

A group of tired, mud-caked British soldiers returning from a spell in the trenches.

CHAPTER EIGHT

The Final Years

We can close our story with a look at what happened to the divisions in 1917 and 1918, particularly those involved in the fighting on the Western Front.

1917

The end of 1916 had seen the Army replacing its Somme casualties with the new influx of recruits in the form of conscripts. But the BEF fought three major battles in 1917 – Arras, Third Ypres and Cambrai – and the resulting casualties could not this time be completely replaced. It was a fact of life on the Western Front that the BEF suffered progressively more casualties as each year of the war came, partly as a result of having more divisions available for operations and partly because more and longer offensive actions were carried out. The casualty figures up to the end of 1917 were:

1914	95,654	(19,927 per month)
1915	296,583	(24,715 per month)
1916	643,249	(53,604 per month)
1917	817,790	(68,149 per month)

British dead awaiting identification and burial. The major battles of 1917 were draining the available manpower.

The total strength of the BEF reached a peak for the whole war in October 1917 with 2,038,105 men – 1,720,077 British (84.4 per cent), 143,974 Canadian (7.1 per cent), 122,141 Australian (6.0 per cent), 29,054 New Zealand (1.4 per cent), 15,488 Indian (0.8 per cent), 7,371 South African (0.4 per cent).★

★ The yearly figures are from *Statistics of the Military Effort*, pages 253-271; the October figures are on a chart facing page 64. The size of the BEF had grown seven and a half times since the first recorded overall figures in the chart of 269,711 for 19 December 1914. The Australian and New Zealand figures are approximate because the chart shows a combined figure; my split is based on the proportions when separate totals were shown on the February 1918 return. The majority of the Indian troops were in their two cavalry divisions.

Captured and wounded further added to the losses in 1917.

But that record BEF manpower figure for October 1917 is misleading. Haig was still keeping three British and two Indian cavalry divisions intact, hoping for an eventual breakthrough and a mobile battle. The cavalry did sometimes take turns at holding trenches, but their men were rarely used in the infantry-attack role. There had also been a steady proliferation of support units – trench-mortar batteries, machine-gun companies, tanks, the Royal Flying Corps – all requiring men, often taken from the infantry battalions.

Those infantry battalions of the BEF emerged from the 1917 battles severely under strength, particularly the British ones. The worst sufferers were the Scottish and Irish units. For the Scots it was because their population was insufficient, even with conscription, to support all of their battalions. Many Irish had held back from volunteering in the days of 1914 and 1915; the absence of conscription in Ireland now created a severe shortage of reinforcements for their units. I would like the reader to be reminded of the statement I made when describing the county regiment system, that once a man had enlisted in an infantry regiment he could normally expect to remain in that regiment for the duration of his service, although he could be moved freely from one battalion to another of the regiment. That situation had been complied

Men from one of the two Indian cavalry divisions serving on the Western Front. They, along with the three British cavalry divisions, were kept intact ready to exploit any breakthrough.

with during the first years of the war with only a few exceptions, but in January 1917 a BEF order was issued that reinforcements earmarked for English regiments at the base camps in France could be transferred to make up shortages in Scots, Welsh and Irish units. The Welsh, with just one division in the BEF, did not have a severe problem. The Scots, with three divisions, did, and many an Englishman was surprised to find himself sent to a kilted battalion.

The Irish problem, with two divisions in the BEF, was, as with most Irish problems, more complex. English reinforcements who had been conscripted were sometimes bitter at being transferred to Irish battalions when Irishmen were not being conscripted. It became a political issue when English MPs carried the protests to Parliament and the practice was curtailed. Both the 16th (Irish) and 36th (Ulster) Divisions had to start reducing the number of their battalions by amalgamations and disbandments and could only remain Irish in content by taking Regular Irish battalions from the Regular divisions in the BEF. The 10th (Irish) Division, now in Palestine, faced the same difficulties. It took in three Irish Regular battalions from the 27th Division at Salonika, but still had to be 'Indianized' in April 1918, having only the three Regular Irish battalions remaining in what had once been a completely New Army division. Even with all these measures, the average Irish battalion, which had been 86 per cent Irish in content in 1914, was only 56 per cent Irish at the end of the war.

Scottish regiments ran short of reinforcements in 1918 and men from English regiments had to be transferred to maintain strengths.

For those interested in statistics, the total wartime enlistment figures for the four home countries, with the percentages of their estimated male populations, are:

England	4,006,158	(24 per cent)
Scotland	557,618	(24 per cent)
Wales	272,924	(22 per cent)
Ireland	134,020	(6 per cent).

The figures are from *Statistics of the Military Effort*, (page 363).

The 1918 Reorganization

The quieter months of the 1917-18 winter gave the authorities the opportunity to produce a solution to the overall shortage of infantry in the British divisions of the BEF. Haig wanted the War Cabinet to send out sufficient troops, which he believed to be available in Britain, to make up the deficiencies. The War Cabinet said this could not be done. Lloyd George, of course, was the leading opponent. The under nineteen-year-old conscripts were all held back as a matter of Government policy, but it was believed that there were many fully fit older men in England who could have been sent. I do not wish to enter into the debate over whether Lloyd George deliberately ordered that the number of potential reinforcements be concealed; one way or another,

Lloyd George with Sir Douglas Haig and General Joffre. Are they trying to convince the Prime Minister of something... the need for more men for the Western Front?

the BEF did not get as many men as Haig wanted. It was a time of great need. The BEF had been forced by French disasters in 1917 to take over further sectors from the French; the Germans, having successfully extricated themselves from a war on two fronts when the Communists in Russia dropped out of the war, were transferring divisions from East to West ready to mount an offensive before the Americans could arrive in strength.

The BEF had to make do with the men it already possessed. A special War Cabinet committee studying the problem of manpower made the drastic suggestion that the British infantry divisions in the BEF should change their long-held organization from three brigades, each of four battalions, to brigades of only three battalions. The French and German Armies had already done this. The men of the one quarter of battalions thus lost would be transferred to bring up to strength the surviving three-quarters of the battalions.

In the winter of 1917-1918 the manpower shortage had become critical and there were real doubts that the BEF could withstand a German attack. Here a group of men crowd around a brazier near Ypres.

The proposed reorganization was approved and the changeover took place in February and early March 1918. Thousands of infantrymen were paraded and told that the units in which they had served, sometimes for several years, would immediately cease to exist. They were divided into groups and marched off to become members of strange battalions, often in different divisions. A total of 115 battalions disappeared completely and thirty-eight more were amalgamated to become nineteen merged battalions. It was decided that Regular battalions and the First Line Territorials would not be affected, so the brunt of the cuts came in the New Army and the Second Line Territorials. The New Army lost the equivalent of about 30 per cent of its battalions and the Second Line Territorials about 60 per cent. The reorganization did nothing to solve the overall shortage of infantry. Not a single extra rifleman became available for trench duty. The reduced number of battalions would now either have to go into the line more often or take over longer frontages.

The effect upon the character of divisions was dramatic. The distinction between Regular and New Army, already weakened by the exchange of brigades after the Battle of Loos and the advent of conscription, almost disappeared. The Territorial divisions were more fortunate because their reorganization took place entirely within their divisions. The Guards were exempt from the cuts, so they transferred a brigade of three battalions to a New Army division, the 31st, the surviving members of whose North Country Pals battalions found

A composite battalion of men from the Leeds and Barnsley Pals, and the Durham Light Infantry prepare to hold the railway line at Merris, 12 April 1918, during the German advance.

themselves sharing a division with what may be regarded as the Army's elite infantry. The Dominion divisions did not reorganize. The Australians had sufficient reinforcements. To make up their shortages, the New Zealanders broke up a reserve brigade in England and the Canadians a complete new division which was assembling in England.

The reorganization produced a small surplus of infantry in most of the British BEF divisions. It was decided not to return these to the base reinforcement camps but to hold them at divisional level in 'Entrenching Battalions' which would help with labouring duties, particularly those on the Fifth Army sector recently taken over from the French where the trench defences were inadequate to face a German attack. In the event of major action these trained infantrymen would immediately be sent back to infantry battalions to replace casualties and the Entrenching Battalions would disappear. (I mention this in detail because people following the careers of soldiers in 1918 sometimes do not understand why a man should suddenly be sent to a strange-sounding unit and just as suddenly leave it.)

The 1918 Battles

The expected German attack took place on 21 March, striking mainly at the extended front of Gough's Fifth Army and forcing back the British and French for nearly twenty miles in two weeks, an undreamt of advance after Allied efforts had succeeded in moving

On 21 March 1918, the Germans attacked on the Western Front and immediately achieved success driving the French and British back twenty miles in two weeks.

forward only a few miles in months of fighting.* The Germans were held at Villers-Bretonneux, but struck again and again elsewhere with huge blows designed to break the British and French before the Americans arrived in strength. Huge amounts of ground were lost. The Allies reeled but never broke. The fighting was ferocious, the casualties enormous. The BEF lost 380,000 men killed, wounded or taken prisoner in the months of March, April and May. The eighteen-year-olds were sent out from England and Lloyd George was forced to release as reinforcements other men he had been hoping to keep from that Western Front which was costing Britain's manhood so dearly. Ten divisions became so weak that they were unfit for front-line service and were reduced to skeleton frameworks. The 14th (Light), 16th (Irish), 25th – reduced to non-active status twice in four months – 30th, 34th, 40th, 50th (Northumbrian) and 66th (2nd East Lancashire) Divisions all had to be taken out of the line in this way and reconstituted before being fit for action again. The 39th and 59th (2nd North Midland) never did recover and finished the war as non-active.

The tide turned. The Americans arrived. The Germans had weakened themselves too much and the naval blockade was starving their homeland. The Allies opened their new offensive on 8 August at Villers-Bretonneux and the steady advance which started on that day continued until the Germans asked for an Armistice in November.

* See the author's *The Kaiser's Battle*, Penguin, for an account of the first day of the German offensive.

Further casualties were suffered as the BEF fell back in front of the German onslaught – but the line remained intact.

Those final battles were almost as costly as the defensive fighting in the Spring. The BEF again suffered nearly 380,000 casualties from 8 August to 11 November, most of them the conscripts, often the eighteen-year-olds, who now provided the majority of men in the infantry units. It was a year of great battles swinging back and forth across France and Belgium, of terrible suffering and death, hardly ever covered in detail by the popular war histories. The BEF, whose worst year for casualties in 1917 had been 817,790 men at a rate of 68,149 per month, now lost 846,861 men, or 81,981 for each of the ten and a third months of 1918!

But the Allies prevailed and those divisions created by Kitchener and once manned by the pre-war Regulars and by those hundreds of thousands of eager volunteers in 1914 and 1915 played a major part in the victory. It was because she had created so many of those divisions, the 'units of currency' of warring armies, that Britain had been able to play that major role and would be able to have a major say in the post-war settlements.

Whether it was all worth it is another matter.

In August 1918 the British and French armies went onto the offensive against the now exhausted German forces. Here British soldiers pursue the 'Hun' following the Battle of Albert.

APPENDIX 1

Wartime Expansion of a Typical County Regiment

In the introduction of this book I set out the pre-war organization of a typical county regiment, the Lincolnshires – the Depot, two Regular battalions, a Special Reserve battalion and two Territorial battalions. This appendix shows how the regiment expanded during the war, where the battalions served and their fatal casualties.

The Depot remained at the New Barracks, Lincoln, taking in recalled Reservists in 1914, forming four New Army battalions in 1914, thereafter playing a mainly admistrative role.

The 1st Battalion, Regulars. In barracks at Portsmouth on the outbreak of war; went with the 3rd Division to France in August 1914. Fought at the Battle of Mons and in almost every subsequent battle on the Western Front. Because of the 2nd Lincolns' links with Bermuda, that island sent two officers and 125 men of its Rifle Volunteer Corps to England with the wish that they serve with the Lincolnshire Regiment and this contingent was then attached to the 1st Battalion in June 1915. The battalion was involved in the exchange of Regular and New Army brigades in November 1915 and was transferred to the 21st Division, in which it remained until the Armistice.

A Lewis gun team of the Lincolns about to go into action at the Hindenburg Line near Epéhy, 18 September 1918.

Fatal casualties: 57 or more officers and 1,508 other ranks, 30.8 per month of active service. Forty of the fatal casualties were Bermudans. (A later note will explain why the officer deaths are understated.)

The 2nd Battalion, Regulars. Returned from peacetime station at Bermuda, joined 8th Division and crossed to France in November 1914. Fought in the Battle of Neuve Chapelle in March 1915 and in most subsequent Western Front battles. Transferred to the 21st Division in the February 1918 reorganization where it served alongside the 1st Battalion for nine months. Fatal casualties: 43 or more officers and 1,455 other ranks, 31.2 per month of active service.

The 3rd Battalion, Special Reserve. Became active at the Depot at Lincoln on the outbreak of war, but almost immediately moved to Grimsby where, in addition to its training duties, it formed part of the home-defence force. In the first weeks of the war it took in the peacetime Special Reservists, continuing their training and then sending them as reinforcements to the 1st and 2nd Battalions. Subsequently it held convalescent wounded from the two Regular battalions and trained wartime recruits sent from the Depot and earmarked as further reinforcements for the Regular battalions. While nominally on the strength of the battalion, 34 officers and 56 other ranks died. The officers, however, were probably those with wartime commissions gazetted to the 3rd Battalion, a more esteemed wartime

Recruiting for the British Army in New York City. This became possible when Congress passed a law permitting Allied governments to call for volunteers from among their subjects, or citizens domiciled in the United States.

commission than those of the New Army or Territorials, and they probably died after being sent to either the 1st or 2nd Battalion. The men who died probably did so in training accidents or through illness, particularly in the 1918 influenza epidemic.

The 4th Battalion, Territorials from South Lincolnshire. Became the 1st/4th Battalion in August 1914 and went to the BEF with the 46th (North Midland) Division in March 1915. Served on the Ypres Salient sector until sent south to take part in the attack on the Hohenzollern Redoubt on 13 October 1915, the last day of the Battle of Loos, and suffering heavy casualties on that day. Sent briefly to Egypt in January 1916 but soon returned to the BEF, continuing to serve there with the 46th Division until the February 1918 reorganization. The battalion transferred to the 59th (2nd North Midland) Division in that reorganization and merged with the 2nd/4th Lincolns, at which time the wartime prefixes were dropped and the combined battalion became simply the 4th Lincolns. After suffering severe casualties in the German offensives of March and April 1918, the 59th Division ceased to be an active division and the remnants of the 4th Battalion were attached to three different divisions before ceasing to exist completely three days before the Armistice. The battalion was reconstituted after the war.

The 5th Battalion, Territorials from North Lincolnshire. Became the 1st/5th Battalion in August 1914. The war record of this battalion was

Making shells in the United States. With America in the war the full might of her production capability became available. Note that the workers are men – in Europe, where men were needed to fight, woman had taken over the roll of armaments production.

similar to that of the 1st/4th, except that it remained in its original form with the 46th Division until the Armistice.

The 2nd/4th Battalion, Second Line Territorials. Formed at Lincoln from the pre-war 4th Battalion men who did not volunteer for overseas service and from the many 1914 and 1915 men who volunteered for the Territorials. It remained at Lincoln until July 1915, training and supplying reinforcements to the 1st/4th Battalion, a duty it would continue to perform until it went to France itself. In 1915 it became part of the 59th (2nd North Midland) Division with which it served in Ireland from April 1916 to January 1917 and then proceeded to the Western Front where it fought in the Battles of Third Ypres and Cambrai. As described above, it merged with the 1st/4th Battalion in the February 1918 reorganization.

The 2nd/5th Battalion, Second Line Territorials. Formed at Grimsby in August 1914 and experienced the same service as the 2nd/4th Battalion, although it remained intact in the February 1918 reorganization and served at the front until the Armistice.

Territorial Casualties. Unfortunately the fatal casualties of the four Territorial battalions are not recorded separately, the 1st/4th and 2nd/4th being combined and the 1st/5th and 2nd/5th being combined. The totals are: 1st/4th and 2nd/4th – 42 officers, 716 other ranks;

A scene in south Russia – a regiment now out of the fight against Germany marches through the streets behind a band which is playing the **Marseillaise.** *They are carrying red flags denoting their support for the revolution. Russia's exit from the war had allowed Germany to release divisions for use on the Western Front. With the imminent arrival of America troops to take part in the fighting in Europe, the Germans tried for all-out victory in the spring of 1918.*

1st/5th and 2nd/5th – 39 officers and 940 other ranks. It is not possible to give the fatal casualties per month of active service but, unlike the Regular and New Army battalions, the officer casualties are accurate.

The Third Line Territorials. The 3rd/4th Battalion was formed at Ipswich in April 1915 from home-service men and later Territorial volunteers. After various moves it became the 4th (Reserve) Battalion in April 1916. The 3rd/5th Battalion formed in the same way, but at Bury St Edmunds, and became the 5th (Reserve) Battalion, but was absorbed by the 4th (Reserve) Battalion in September 1916. During these years, these units were training reinforcements for the active service Territorial battalions of the regiment and also acting as home-defence units. In July 1917, with Territorial volunteering no longer being allowed, the 4th (Reserve) Battalion ceased to be part of the Lincolnshire Regiment.

6th Battalion, New Army. Formed from early wartime volunteers at the Depot in August 1914 and became part of the K1 11th (Northern) Division. Sent to the Mediterranean and took part in the 6 August 1915 landing at Suvla Bay, Gallipoli. Then served in Egypt until July 1916 when the division moved to the Western Front, taking part in the Battle of the Somme in September. The battalion remained with the division on the Western Front until the Armistice. Fatal casualties: 13 or more officers and 659 other ranks, 20.6 per month of service in a war theatre.

Major-General John Pershing, Commander-in-Chief of the American Expeditionary Force, arrived in England in June 1917 with his staff of 53 officers and 146 men. A British general greeted Pershing on behalf of the British War Office. The guard of honour was provided by the Royal Welsh Fusiliers. It was noted that the soldiers were young teenagers. General Pershing eventually arrived at Boulogne where he was welcomed by the French Government.

7th Battalion, New Army. Formed at the Depot in September 1914, and became part of the K2 17th (Northern) Division. Crossed to France in July 1915, took part in the Battle of the Somme and all of the division's battles until the Armistice.

Fatal casualties: 37 or more officers and 928 other ranks, 24.2 per month of active service.

8th Battalion, New Army. Formed at the Depot in September 1914 and became part of the K3 21st Division. Crossed to France in September 1915 and was almost immediately involved in the Battle of Loos when two untried New Army divisions were thrown into the battle on the second morning. Transferred to the 37th Division in July 1916, fighting on the Somme and in all of the 37th Division's battles until the Armistice.

Fatal casualties: 33 or more officers and 871 other ranks, 23.8 per month of active service.

9th Battalion, New Army. Formed at Lincoln in November 1914 and intended for active service in one of the K4 group of divisions but transformed to reserve status when the 10th Battalion was formed by private initiative at Grimsby. The battalion remained in England, most of the time at a camp on Cannock Chase, supplying reinforcements, mostly for the 6th, 7th and 8th Battalions.

Troopship Leviathan, *formerly the German passenger liner* Vaterland, *leaving for France with around 12,000 soldiers aboard, May 1918.*

10th Battalion, New Army. Raised in Grimsby by local initiative, originally intended as a company of old boys of the local grammar school (later Wintringham Grammar School) to be offered to the local Territorials, but growing to battalion size mostly with men from the Grimsby area but being made up to full strength with men from other parts of the county and from other areas. Became known as The Grimsby Chums – the only 'Chums' battalion in the Pals movement. Taken over by the Army in August 1915 as part of the K4 34th Division. Crossed to France in January 1916 and suffered severely in its first attack near the Lochnagar Crater at La Boisselle on the opening day of the Battle of the Somme. Continued with the 34th Division until May 1918 when, after again suffering severe casualties in the German offensives, it was no longer strong enough for active service and became a training cadre and a lines-of-communication unit until the Armistice.

Fatal casualties: 22 or more officers and 788 other ranks, 28.7 per month while active in the BEF as a fighting unit.

11th Battalion. Formed at Lincoln from the reserve company of the 10th Battalion in October 1915, just before the 10th went to France. Remained in England, training recruits predominantly for the 10th Battalion and carrying out home-defence duties, but the battalion ceased to be part of the Lincolnshire Regiment in September 1916. Four men died during the 'Lincolns' existence.

An enthusiastic reception for Americans arriving in Paris – here seen marching down the Rue de Rivoli.

12th (Labour) Battalion. Formed at Brocklesby Park in July 1916 with men considered unfit for front-line service. Crossed to France and employed in the BEF until being disbanded and becoming companies of the Labour Corps in April 1917. Five men died during the war.

13th Battalion, Territorials. Formed in January 1917 at Bath from a 'Provisional Battalion' which had been holding home-service men from various Territorial units. The battalion served in the 72nd (Home Service) Division in the Ipswich area but left the division in mid-1917 and was disbanded in October. No fatal casualties are recorded. This battalion may have had only a nominal link with the Lincolnshire Regiment.

1st Garrison Battalion. Formed in September 1915 from men unfit for front-line service and went to India the following month. Two officers are recorded as dying.

2nd (Home Service) Garrison Battalion. Formed in May 1916 at North Coates but became part of the Royal Defence Corps in 1917. No fatal casualties recorded.

Summary

The Lincolnshire Regiment grew from five battalions on the outbreak of war to a total of nineteen battalions, eleven of which

American troops marching through London and greeted by a huge crowd in Trafalgar Square. A vital reinforcement of manpower for the Western Front had arrived.

engaged in front-line fighting, entirely on the Western Front except for the 6th Battalion's five months at Gallipoli. The regiment's overall war dead are given as 394 officers and 8,042 other ranks in *Officers Died in the Great War* and *Soldiers Died in the Great War*, but the battalion figures only come to 328 officers and 7,938 men, a shortfall of 66 officers and 104 other ranks. Of the officers, 33 are known to have died while temporarily attached to other infantry regiments or while serving in the RFC/RAF or other units, but the other 33 were probably with Regular or New Army battalions of their regiment and have not been properly recorded as such. Some of the 104 extra other ranks deaths were probably with trench-mortar batteries or machine-gun companies when those units were created with battalion personnel or, like the extra officers, were battalion men who have not been properly recorded as such. The number of men wounded or evacuated sick or taken prisoner may have been about 18,000, making a total casualty list for the Lincolnshire Regiment of over 26,000.

If the reader thinks that this catalogue of one regiment's wartime experience is lengthy and complicated, let her or him bear in mind that the same thing happened in sixty-six other county-type regiments and wonder at that great achievement by the British Army in expanding its strength in the First World War.

Prisoners near Méricourt l'Abbé, 8 August 1918. General Ludendorff referred to that day as 'The Black Day of the German Army'. They are passing a section of anti-aircraft guns.

APPENDIX 2

Wartime Record and Fatal Casualties of Infantry Regiments

In the tables below, the central column of figures shows the total number of wartime battalions in a regiment and the number of them which saw active service on at least one fighting front. So, in the Grenadier Guards, '5/4' indicates a total of five battalions, of which four saw active service. The right-hand column shows the number of Grenadier fatal casualties – 4,658, with average deaths in the active service battalions – 1,141 – in brackets.

The totals of fatal casualties are taken from *Officers Died in the Great War* and *Soldiers Died in the Great War*. Because approximately 2 per cent of deaths occurred when soldiers were not serving in one of a regiment's active service battalions, the average figures used for such battalion deaths are calculated as 98 per cent of a regiment's total recorded deaths. It should be remembered that the number of additional casualties from wounds, sickness and being taken prisoner were approximately twice as many as the numbers killed, but exact figures for these are not available.

Foot Guard Regiments

Grenadier	5/4	4,658 (1,141)
Coldstream	5/4	3,810 (933)
Scots	3/2	2,843 (1,393)
Irish	3/2	2,191 (1,074)
Welsh	2/1	853 (836)

British troops prepare to advance through the Hindenburg Line near Bellicourt, September 1918. MkV tanks are on the skyline and there are some German prisoners.

English Line Regiments

London	88/55	29,074 (518)
Northumberland Fusiliers	51/25	17,005 (667)
Royal Fusiliers	47/23	16,321 (695)
Manchester	44/24	14,124 (577)
King's (Liverpool)	49/22	13,795 (615)
Lancashire Fusiliers	31/21	13,462 (628)
West Yorkshire	35/19	13,005 (671)
King's Royal Rifle Corps	28/16	12,848 (787)
Middlesex	49/23	12,590 (536)
Durham Light Infantry	42/20	12,557 (615)
Rifle Brigade	28/12	11,804 (964)
Royal Warwickshire	30/16	11,358 (696)
Sherwood Foresters	33/18	11,298 (615)
King's Own Yorkshire Light Infantry	24/12	9,450 (772)
Worcestershire	22/12	9,412 (769)
York and Lancaster	22/14	8,956 (627)
Essex	30/10	8,935 (876)
Lincolnshire	19/10	8,436 (827)
Cheshire	38/14	8,413 (589)
Duke of Wellington's (West Riding)	22/13	8,131 (613)
Gloucestershire	24/15	8,102 (529)
Queen's (West Surrey)	27/10	7,892 (773)
Loyal North Lancashire	21/11	7,686 (685)

It was becoming obvious to the ordinary soldier that the end was in sight. You can almost see the relief in the faces of these men posed around a captured German 4.2 inch gun.

East Yorkshire	19/10	7,552 (740)
Hampshire	32/13	7,515 (567)
Green Howards (The Yorkshire)	24/11	7,503 (668)
Royal Sussex	26/10	7,096 (695)
Leicestershire	22/11	7,028 (626)
Royal West Kent	18/10	6,958 (682)
Royal Berkshire	16/8	6,942 (850)
Suffolk	23/9	6,851 (746)
Border	16/8	6,762 (828)
East Lancashire	17/11	6,647 (592)
King's Own Royal Lancaster	18/10	6,478 (635)
Bedfordshire	21/7	6,424 (900)
South Staffordshire	17/9	6,357 (692)
East Surrey	18/8	6,356 (779)
Devonshire	29/10	6,128 (601)
Northamptonshire	13/6	6,075 (992)
Norfolk	19/7	6,026 (844)
The Buffs (East Kent)	15/6	5,680 (928)
Oxford and Bucks Light Infantry	18/10	5,679 (557)
North Staffordshire	19/9	5,608 (611)
South Lancashire	21/12	5,433 (444)
Wiltshire	10/6	4,886 (798)
Somerset Light Infantry	18/8	4,748 (582)
King's Shropshire Light Infantry	12/7	4,733 (663)

A bugler blows the 'Cease Fire!' The Great War ended at 11am, November 11, 1918. Irish Guards at the Mons Gate, Maubeuge, liberated after fifty months.

Duke of Cornwall's Light Infantry	15/8	4,280 (524)
Dorsetshire	11/6	3,929 (642)
Honourable Artillery Company	3/2	981 (481)
Hertfordshire	4/1	852 (835)
Cambridgeshire	4/1	844 (827)
Herefordshire	3/1	494 (484)

It should be appreciated that large numbers of wartime recruits from the three Territorial-only counties at the foot of the above table enlisted in regiments of neighbouring counties which had Regular and New Army battalions.

Scottish Line Regiments

Royal Scots	34/13	11,209 (845)
Highland Light Infantry	33/14	9,998 (700)
Gordon Highlanders	23/9	8,963 (976)
Seaforth Highlanders	17/8	8,419 (1,031)
Black Watch	22/9	8,378 (912)
Argyll and Sutherland Highlanders	26/10	6,875 (674)
King's Own Scottish Borderers	14/7	6,861 (961)
Cameronians (Scottish Rifles)	27/10	6,670 (654)
Royal Scots Fusiliers	18/7	5,934 (831)
Cameron Highlanders	14/6	5,884 (961)

Homeward bound, the 'great adventure' over – troops at a London railway terminus queuing to exchange their French francs for Sterling.

Irish Line Regiments

Royal Irish Rifles	21/13	7,005 (528)
Royal Inniskilling Fusiliers	13/9	5,772 (629)
Royal Dublin Fusiliers	11/7	4,778 (669)
Royal Irish Fusiliers	14/7	3,375 (473)
Royal Munster Fusiliers	11/6	2,835 (463)
Royal Irish	10/4	2,603 (638)
Leinster	7/4	2,067 (506)
Connaught Rangers	6/4	1,998 (490)

Welsh Line Regiments

Royal Welsh Fusiliers	40/16	9,957 (610)
Welsh	35/17	7,775 (448)
South Wales Borderers	21/10	5,732 (562)
Monmouth	10/3	1,584 (517)

Summary of Regiments

Foot Guards	18/13	14,355 (1,082)
English	1,305/650	437,499 (660)
Scottish	228/93	79,191 (834)
Irish	93/54	30,433 (552)
Welsh	106/46	25,048 (534)

British regiments contained 1,750 wartime battalions, of which 856 saw active service. Fatal casualties were 586,526 – 672 per active service battalion

British troops arriving from Salonika having survived the worst war in the history of mankind.

Highest Average Active Service Battalion Deaths

Scots Guards	1,393
Grenadier Guards	1,141
Irish Guards	1,074
Seaforth Highlanders	1,031
Northamptonshire	992
Gordon Highlanders	976
Rifle Brigade	964
Cameron Highlanders	961
King's Own Scottish Borderers	961
Coldstream Guards	933
The Buffs (East Kent)	928
Black Watch	912

The figures in the above two tables are interesting but should be treated with caution. The deaths of fighting battalions depended largely on a regiment's mix of Regular, New Army and First and Second Line Territorial battalions. The New Army and, particularly, the Second Line Territorials arrived at battle fronts later in the war and thus were likely to suffer fewer casualties. The Guards had no New Army or Territorial battalion. The Scots Guards had no wartime-raised battalions at all, which explains their position at the top of the second table. The Rifle Brigade had no Territorials. None of the Scottish Second Line

Troops of the British Army of Occupation marching with fixed bayonets through the streets of Cologne.

Territorial battalions nor those of the Northamptons and the Buffs reached fighting fronts.

A closer examination of individual *battalion* casualties shows that the Scottish First Line Territorial and New Army battalions suffered particularly heavy losses, some of the Territorials as emergency reinforcements with the BEF in 1914 and then with the hard fighting 51st (Highland) Division; the Scottish New Army battalions suffered heavily with the 9th and 15th (Scottish) Divisions at Loos. The highest English county regiment figures are in the Northamptons. Examination of their losses shows the 1st Battalion with exceptionally high figures of at least 1,665 deaths, the result of long service on the Western Front with the 1st Division, including the disaster on 10 July 1917 when the Germans overran two battalions in the sand dunes next to the North Sea at Nieuport. Another Northampton battalion with extraordinary losses was the 6th, with at least 1,230 deaths, attributable to its service with the 18th (Eastern) Division which, because of complete success in its early battles on the Somme in 1916, was repeatedly used as an attacking division in following years.

The Channel Islands

The preceding tables of casualties include every infantry regiment of the British Army in 1914-18 with one exception – the wartime raised Royal Guernsey Light Infantry. Our story ends with a description of how the men of Guernsey and its sister island, Jersey, made their

Officers and men of the 15th Argyll and Sutherland Highlanders on their last parade before demobilization.

wartime contribution.

The Channel Islands had no Regulars or Territorials in 1914, only Militias – leftovers from before the 1908 Haldane Reforms, but their members were probably trained and equipped as well as the mainland Territorials. Many of the militiamen volunteered for service with the British Army on the outbreak of war and we have seen how three company-sized contingents – two from Guernsey and one from Jersey – went to the 16th (Irish) Division where they served, being supplied with reinforcement drafts from the islands, until the Irish battalions were disbanded later in the war. Guernsey suffered 95 to 98 (figures vary) fatal casualties and Jersey 79 with the original Irish battalions until the disbandments; more were suffered when the men were transferred to other units afterwards. All of these casualties are contained in the relevant Irish regiments' figures above.

Guernsey's artillery militiamen formed the 9th (Scottish) Division's Divisional Ammunition Column (nearly 400 men served, with 15 fatal casualties) and the island's Engineers Militia provided a Royal Engineers company in France (143 served, 4 died). In 1918, 232 Guernsey quarrymen served in two Royal Engineer quarrying companies in France; one man was killed in an air raid.

When Britain introduced conscription, Guernsey and Jersey, independently and separately, followed. The Militias were suspended and men were conscripted directly into the British Army. In the case of the Guernseymen, they went into a newly formed battalion, the 1st

The Lord Mayor taking the salute of a contingent of London soldiers in the post-war victory parade.

Royal Guernsey Light Infantry, which served in the 29th Division from October 1917 until April 1918, fighting at Cambrai where it suffered 40 per cent casualties and then against the German Offensive on the Lys where casualties reached nearly 80 per cent. Despite being made up with men from the North Staffords, the battalion left the 29th Division and became the guard unit at GHQ at Montreuil. The battalion's fatal casualties were 333 men. Guernsey's war dead numbered at least 450 in all of these units, plus an unknown number among other local men who volunteered to serve directly with mainland units. Some men from both islands chose to join the French Army.

Jersey's conscripts did not have their own unit, but were sent to various units of the British Army where their deaths are included in the totals of their respective regiments. It is known that Jersey's total war dead numbered 878.

The Victory Parade passes the Cenotaph in Whitehall. Memorials sprang up throughout this country commemorating the sacrifice of the thousands who had lost their lives serving in the Great War.

ACKNOWLEDGEMENTS

I would like to express my thanks to several friends who have carried out research tasks for me. First is my battlefield touring partner, Mike Hodgson of Tumby Woodside, who spent much time accessing his CD Roms for regimental and battalion casualty figures, which was a great help to this electronically illiterate author. My other friendly helpers I place in alphabetical order, but I am equally grateful to all: Tom Brophy of Rochdale, Philip Curme of Swavesey in Cambridgeshire, Tim Dunce of Bovey Tracey in Devon, Norbert Krüger of Essen, John Morcombe of High Wycombe, Dick Rayner of Spixworth near Norwich, Margaret and Alan Stansfield of Elland, Yorks, James Taylor of Clonard, Great Wexford, and Ken Tough of Guernsey.

Next, many thanks must go to my part-time secretary cum word-processor expert, Margaret Gardner of Boston, who had taken my word that I had retired from writing books and became fully employed elsewhere; she has had to give up many weekends to produce this typescript with her usual skill.

I would also like to thank the historians of the Royal Marines (Major V.M. Bentinck) and of the following regiments for answering my queries: Grenadier Guards (Captain D. Mason), Royal Lincolnshire

Immediately following the war's end, pilgrimages began as relatives set out to visit the graves of lost loved ones and the locations where they gave up their lives. The rubble that once was the Belgian town of Ypres by the British artist Matania.

(Captain John Lee), Devonshire (Lieutenant-Colonel J. Mitchell), Royal Leicestershire (Colonel F.A.H. Swallow), Worcestershire (Lieutenant-Colonel C.P. Love), Royal Hampshire (Lieutenant-Colonel C.D. Darroch), Dorset (Major L.D. Brown), Middlesex (Major A.E.F. Waldron – 84 years old!) and Royal Green Jackets (Colonel I.H. McCausland).

Many thanks to the staff of The Department of Printed Books at the Imperial War Museum for research help.

Finally, thanks to my wife, Mary, for help with the index.

Bibliography

War Establishments for 1907-1908, HMSO (original price 'Eightpence'!)

History of the Great War, Order of Battle of Divisions, complied by Major A.F. Becke in five parts and originally published by His Majesty's Stationary Office between 1937 and 1945. Part 1 was reprinted by Sherwood Press, Nottingham, date unknown; Part 2A, same publisher, 1987; Parts 2B (1988), 3A and 3B (dates unknown) by Ray Westlake, Malpas, Gwent.

Officers Died in the Great War, Parts 1 and 2, HMSO, 1919; reprinted by Samson Books Ltd, London SE1 2BT, 1975.

Soldiers Died in the Great War, multiple volumes, HMSO, 1921; the version used by Mike Hodgson was the CD Rom by Naval and Military Press, Dallington, Sussex, 1998.

Gruesome battlefield debris that could still be found in 1919 within the infamous Ypres Salient.

Statistics of the Military Effort of the British Empire during the Great War: 1914-1920, HMSO, 1922.

British Regiments, 1914-18, by Brigadier E.A. James; Samson Books, London, 1978.

Orange, Green and Khaki, The Story of the Irish Regiments in the Great War, 1914-18, by Tom Johnstone; Gill and Macmillan, Dublin, 1992.

Diex Aix: God Help Us, The Guernseymen who Marched Away, 1914-18, by Major Edwin Parks; Guernsey Museums and Galleries, 1992.

Island of Jersey, The Great War, 1914-1919, published privately in Jersey, 1919.

The 18th (Eastern) Division Memorial at Trônes Wood on the Somme commemorating the division's fallen during the war.

Bernafay Wood British Cemetery on the Somme in 1919.

ORGANIZED BATTLEFIELD TOURS

Martin Middlebrook and his business partner, Mike Hodgson, run a small organization that takes parties of visitors to the First World War battlefields, different tours covering the whole length of the Western Front from the Belgian Coast to Verdun. Every two or three years a tour also visits Normandy, to cover the 1944 invasion beaches and battle area, and to Gallipoli, to cover the 1915-16 campaign.

The tour parties are kept small – normally under thirty people – in order not to become unwieldy and to allow a more personal service to be provided. Travel is by a small Mercedes coach starting from Boston, Lincolnshire, which allows people from the north to stay overnight in Boston at reasonable expense; there are other pick-up points on the way to the Channel ports. Tours last from four to six days and are 'non-smoking' (people are expected not to smoke while in the company of other members of the group).

Further details can be obtained from:
Middlebrook-Hodgson Battlefield Tours,
Lancaster Farm,
TUMBY WOODSIDE,
PE22 7SP
Phones: 01205-364555 (Martin Middlebrook) and 01526-342249 (Mike Hodgson), Fax: 01526-345249

Life returns to normal – for a while – until the next time.

Index